PRAISE F

In these days when chaos seems to drive the evening news cycle and broken relationships seem to be more the norm than not, when we stop for a minute—just stop—the soul's reach for God breaks through. That longing to touch and be touched by God rises from the soul of every human. Even so, God often feels unreachable. Tony Kriz offers a new generation guidance on its journey to encounter God. Raw, honest, and wise, Kriz's narrative reminded me to cherish those awe-inspiring moments when God came in close. Remember them. Soak them in. They are fuel for our journey—especially when God feels aloof.

—LISA SHARON HARPER, SENIOR DIRECTOR OF
MOBILIZING, SOJOURNERS & SOJO.NET

Tony is a prophet of our times. His story is mixed with reality and hope that draws you to know God in a deep and realistic way. This book presents the mystery so that it appeals it to those who may find themselves questioning where to find it and into a space to actually find *him*.

—LEROY BARBER, GLOBAL EXECUTIVE
DIRECTOR OF WORD MADE FLESH

Like having a late-night conversation with a good friend where no topic is off-limits, and no question is too difficult to ask. Kriz's engaging candor offers an invitation to travel with him on life's journey with the Silent Divine, a mysterious yet merciful God who often seems to hide.

—SARAH THEBARGE, AUTHOR OF *THE INVISIBLE GIRLS*

Televangelists and preachers make out that God is ever-present and easily accessible, but the stark reality is, at best, we perceive God fitfully, partially, and mysteriously. Tony Kriz, brutally honest and sincerely compassionate, invites us into the mystery of the God who appears aloof, but who beckons us through the fog of life.

—MICHAEL FROST, MORLING COLLEGE, SYDNEY

Tony Kriz writes like he lives. He tells the truth and then lives it.

—Dr. Andrea Cook, President of
Warner Pacific College

Tony's raw and compelling storytelling drives the reader off the beaten path of intellect and into the rocky terrain of our hearts' greatest pain, loss, and unorthodox hope. This book is liberating in that it asks the questions so many of us have about the not-so-tangible-presence of God, yet find ourselves too fearful to ask. Tony doesn't offer all the answers, but gives us the freedom to see, experience, and communicate with God in ways we wouldn't have considered. A must-read for us everyday folks committed to stumbling toward Jesus.

—Jon Huckins, Cofounding Director of
The Global Immersion Project and Author
of *Thin Places: Six Postures for Creating
and Practicing Missional Community*

It's a breath of fresh air to come upon a book like *Aloof*. Tony Kriz challenges paint-by-numbers conventionality with brave honesty about doubt, struggle, and the elusiveness of God—a struggle many Christians experience but few are willing to acknowledge so candidly. Just as Tony has made a friend out of a "doubting Thomas" like me with his kindness, openness, and infectious new ways of seeing things, he is bound to make legions of literary friends with his remarkable new book.

—Tom Krattenmaker, USA Contributing Columnist
and Author of *The Evangelicals You Don't Know*

Tony Kriz unlocks memories, mystery, and imagination in this invitation to see the divine breath which is invisible to so many, though it surrounds all of us every day. A masterful storyteller and whimsical writer, Kriz provokes his readers to live into the reality of the silence of God, and wait in anticipation for the times when we're surprised by the tangible realities of *God with us*.

—Michael Kimpan, Executive Director
of The Marin Foundation

One of Tony Kriz's greatest gifts is navigating complex—even confounding—concepts like theology and theodicy in relatable, digestible ways. He does so once again with grace, humor, and vulnerable transparency in *Aloof*.

—CHRISTIAN PIATT, AUTHOR OF *POSTCHRISTIAN:*
WHAT'S LEFT? CAN WE FIX IT? DO WE CARE?

Honest, transparent, and relevant, *Aloof* is one of the rare books that, while telling someone else's story, helps unpack your own spiritual narrative along the way. A must-read.

—KEN WYTSMA, AUTHOR OF *PURSUING JUSTICE* AND
THE GRAND PARADOX: THE MESSINESS OF LIFE, THE
MYSTERY OF GOD AND THE NECESSITY OF FAITH

If you are looking for perfect, sanitized stories of people who make all the right choices or who never waver in the face of tragedy, this is not the book for you. If you gain strength by stories of others who search for God and sometimes still feel like the kid who is losing at hide-and-seek, this book will encourage you that you do not search alone.

—MICKY SCOTTBEY JONES, TRANSFORM NETWORK, PATHEOS
EMERGING VOICES BLOG, RED LETTER CHRISTIANS

Tony explores the mystery behind the "presence of God" in our lives, pulling apart the expectations of God's presence that have potentially been taught to us. A truly transparent, thoughtful, and honest memoir, *Aloof* is Tony's account of the seasons and journeys of God's presence in his life.

—RACHEL GOBLE, PRESIDENT OF THE SOLD PROJECT

Tony takes us on a powerful, vulnerable journey through his spiritual life, from a young boy to a man. We are invited to walk with him as he wrestles with a God who at times does not seem near enough, tangible enough, or intimate enough. His unnerving honesty reveals the questions found deep in our own hearts, and will ultimately help us find hope in the mercy of God who remains constant through our struggle and invites us to rest.

—KEVIN PALAU, PRESIDENT OF THE LUIS
PALAU EVANGELISTIC ASSOCIATION

Reading *Aloof* is a pleasure. People will debate the ideas—is there a God or not?—but no one will put this book down feeling cheated. It is a work of art.

—FRANK SCHAEFFER, AUTHOR OF *WHY I AM AN ATHEIST WHO BELIEVES IN GOD*

Beautifully written, heartbreaking, revealing, and honest, *Aloof* gives us hope that in the end, God will reveal himself and take each of us by the hand.

—MATT MIKALATOS, AUTHOR OF *THE FIRST TIME WE SAW HIM*

Tony Kriz articulates his experiences of God's aloofness so the rest of us can find the language and freedom to articulate our own. Like our best poets, prophets, and mystics, he looks into the darkness and tells us what he sees—and what he doesn't. The result is a searingly honest but ultimately hopeful book about a "God who hides" but then is occasionally, suddenly, briefly, mysteriously, and wonderfully *there*.

—JOHN PATTISON, COAUTHOR OF *SLOW CHURCH*

With raw honesty, disarming vulnerability, and faith-filled hope, Tony Kriz creates a space for us to rediscover the divine mystery that God is at times perhaps most powerfully and intentionally at work in the moments when it feels like he's left the building.

—JOSHUA RYAN BUTLER, AUTHOR OF *THE SKELETONS IN GOD'S CLOSET*

Can you really trust God when he is silent? It's an age-old question. Easy to answer for those who've not experienced silence. With the precision of a surgeon and the tenderness of a wounded spirit, Tony walks us through his prism to find where God really lives.

—HON. JASON A. ATKINSON, OREGON STATE SENATOR, PRODUCER OF *A RIVER BETWEEN US*

An anguished search for the hand of God in the raucous uncertainty and redemptive community that otherwise attends us.

—STEVE DUIN, COLUMNIST FOR *THE OREGONIAN*

The ordinary doesn't usually feel sacramental, but that doesn't mean God isn't closer, much closer than you think. I'm grateful for this wise and honest memoir that is more than a reminder, it's a literary companion on the winding journey of life with God.

—TIM SOERENS, COFOUNDING DIRECTOR OF THE PARISH COLLECTIVE AND COAUTHOR OF *THE NEW PARISH: HOW NEIGHBORHOOD CHURCHES ARE TRANSFORMING MISSION, DISCIPLESHIP AND COMMUNITY*

Whenever Tony's talking or writing, I lean in. He gives voice to the questions many of us struggle to articulate—either through fear of what others will think, or because we just don't have the words—and invites us to sit with them a while. Not necessarily to find answers, but because our questions have much to teach us, if we'll let them. He tells great stories with humorous, evocative, and at times delectable prose. Often right before he punches you in the gut.

—SEAN GLADDING, AUTHOR OF *THE STORY OF GOD, THE STORY OF US* AND *TEN: WORDS OF LIFE FOR AN ADDICTED, COMPULSIVE, CYNICAL, DIVIDED AND WORN-OUT CULTURE*

Tony says this is not a book of theology; don't believe it. It's the best kind of theology: the lived kind. So while you're laughing and crying (sometimes on the same page), just know that you're drinking deeper than you may realize from the wisdom in these words.

—SHANE BLACKSHEAR, HOST OF SEMINARY DROPOUT (PODCAST) AND BLOGGER AT SHANEBLACKSHEAR.COM

The hiddenness of God—despite being a touchy, if not out-of-bounds, topic for many Christians—is anything but ambiguous in the pages of the Bible. God arrives as the hidden One. What Kriz has done here is nothing short of a masterpiece.

—A.J. SWOBODA, PROFESSOR, PASTOR, AND AUTHOR OF *A GLORIOUS DARK* AND *INTRODUCING EVANGELICAL ECOTHEOLOGY*

My friend Tony Kriz always asks courageous questions with unchartered answers. He understands the sacredness and power of story and his style reminds me of someone . . . sometimes his words are in red.

—RANDY WOODLEY, AUTHOR OF *SHALOM AND THE COMMUNITY OF CREATION: AN INDIGENOUS VISION*

ALOOF

FIGURING OUT LIFE WITH
A GOD WHO HIDES

TONY KRIZ

W Publishing Group

An Imprint of Thomas Nelson

Published in Nashville, Tennessee, by Thomas Nelson. Thomas Nelson is a registered trademark of Thomas Nelson, Inc.

Thomas Nelson, Inc. titles may be purchased in bulk for educational, business, fundraising, or sales promotional use. For information, please e-mail SpecialMarkets@ ThomasNelson.com.

Scripture quotations marked MSG are from the The Message by Eugene H. Peterson. © 1993, 1994, 1995, 1996, 2000. Used by permission of NavPress Publishing Group. All rights reserved.

Scripture quotations marked NASB are from the NEW AMERICAN STANDARD BIBLE®. © The Lockman Foundation 1960, 1962, 1963, 1968, 1971, 1972, 1973, 1975, 1977. Used by permission.

Scripture quotations marked NIV are from the THE HOLY BIBLE, NEW INTERNATIONAL VERSION®, NIV ® Copyright © 1973, 1978, 1984, 2010 by Biblica, Inc.™ Used by permission. All rights reserved worldwide.

Scripture quotations marked NKJV are taken from the New King James Version. © 1982 by Thomas Nelson, Inc. Used by permission. All rights reserved.

Library of Congress Cataloging-in-Publication Data

Kriz, Tony.
Aloof : figuring out life with a God who hides / by Tony Kriz.
pages cm
Includes bibliographical references.
ISBN 978-0-8499-4740-7 (trade paper)
1. Presence of God--Miscellanea. 2. Hidden God--Miscellanea. I. Title.
BT180.P6K75 2015
231'.4--dc23
2014022309

Printed in the United States of America

14 15 16 17 RRD 5 4 3 2 1

For Ransom

CONTENTS

PART 3: INTO THE WORLD

PART 4: REANIMATION

AUTHOR'S NOTE

IN THE FOLLOWING PAGES, you are going to find my stories. They are written with my heart as well as my memory. I am sure that my memories are flawed, made hazy by time. I know some memories are incomplete, so gaps are filled by research and carefully discerned imagination. I have labored to tell these stories accurately. I have tried to represent my friends well. Out of respect, some names have been changed. In a hope to be readable, some details have been omitted and a few conversations have been consolidated.

However, it's also worth noting that historical accuracy is an important but secondary goal.

———

Storytelling is an important spiritual practice. It may even be essential to the way we humans have been designed.

You see, our stories are precious things. They are the foundation of our beliefs. They are the fuel of our hope. My soul has forgotten most of my stories. They have long ago drifted away into the fog.

However, there are a precious few that my soul vigorously holds on to. Why? I believe that part of the reason is to undergird my belief.

Let me explain it another way. The most important question is not, do I remember my memories accurately? (Even though I have striven to do just that in these pages.) The most important thing, in regard to my personal spiritual formation, is to ask these questions:

Why have I chronicled these particular memories?

Why have I remembered them the way I have remembered them?

How do they help me live and believe as I do?

This is the process of narrative spiritual formation. I have built a museum of memories in my soul. In the following pages, I am going to give you a personally guided tour of that museum. The portion of the museum we are going to focus on is the wing that answers the question, What do I believe about God's presence . . . and God's absence? Also the questions, Why does God hide from us? and Why do I hide from God?

I hope that my often-raw musings introduce categories of the God-encounter that are thought provoking. My greater hope, though, is that you are able to blow the dust off your own museum of God-memories. I hope that you will be able to bounce your own stories off of mine and through that process better understand why you have curated the particular memories you have.

It may be a cliché, but I really want this book to be *for you* and in an odd way, *about you*.

There is, admittedly, at least one confusing dichotomy in these pages. Is this a book about God's absence or a book about God's presence? I believe the answer to that either-or question is yes. It is an exploration of God's hiddenness, through a discussion of God's occasionally suspicious presence. I hope, by book's end, you will see how each of these ideas relies upon the other.

This is not a systematic theology text. I am not trying to cover every aspect of God's character or the avenues of divine engagement.

In fact, I never once asked myself, "What angles am I missing?" This is a memoir exploration. I am surfing the waves of my unique experiences around the question of God's presence. Nothing more. If there are important questions that I have not addressed here, then those offer wonderful opportunities for you to add a chapter to the dialogue. If you do, I hope it comes from your very real and rarely simplistic experiences with the Divine.

That being said, my hope is that this book (and most all of my writings) offers an honest and explorative tone, such that anyone from any faith background would feel fully invited into the conversation at hand.

And now, I hope you enjoy *Aloof.* May it speak to you. May it help you curate your personal museum of faith memories. May it embolden your life with God.

Let the epiphanies come,
—TONY KRIZ

INTRODUCTION

THIS IS A BOOK about someone I love. It is a testimony really, a testimony to that love and also to my hate.

I have heard it said that to love is to hate. To have the capacity to love something, you must have the capacity to hate it as well. That is certainly true when I think of my father, who died last year. It is true of my wife, who endures my insanities. It is also true of all my best friends . . . Kevin, Jeff, Cori, Jonathan . . . the list goes on and on.

Sometimes I wonder if this someone, the person that this book is about, actually exists. Sometimes I wonder if I made him up. If I did, I assure you that I came upon this deception honestly. I did not concoct this someone alone. Most everyone who contributed to forming me as a person collaborated, maybe even conspired, to convince me that this someone is true . . . my beautiful allusive someone.

This someone, imaginary or otherwise, has walked with me every stage of my life. There are long stretches where he is wholly silent and at least a few moments where he is as loud as a hangover. That is how it is with my secret someone.

My someone, of course, is God.

My hope is to testify honestly about my someone. I want to tell you about some of our adventures together and about our hateful silences.

What are we to do with a companion who hides?

I have been told all throughout my life about God. I have been told that God is loving and powerful and always with us. The stories were most often triumphant. People cooed, often swaying on stage in front of guitars and a plexiglass-encircled drum set. They cooed about this ever-close God, this ever-speaking God, this ever-tangible God. The words were beautiful and inspiring and made me want to sway along too, yet when the service was over . . .

. . . Back out on the street, I would look for the close, the speaking, the tangible companion we had just been singing about, but he was nowhere to be seen. I would reach out with my emotions to feel, well, anything. My emotions would not return to me, finding nothing to bounce off of, like a lost sonar ping.

"God, are you there?"

This question is as natural to the human experience as, Why is the sky blue? or Why am I here? or Will I ever find true love?

The equation seems logical enough. It is so simple that even a child could conceive its parts. The equation embodies a mystery that has been haunting me most all of my life.

It goes something like this:

1. If God is all-powerful, just as the pages of the Bible teach me,
2. If God loves me and truly wants to know me, so much so that he would introduce himself with names like "Father" and "Emmanuel" ("God with Us"), and
3. If God is an effective and apt communicator, so much

so that he would invent language, make us relational
beings, and adopt the name "The Word,"

Then why does he hide from me most of the time?

To make matters even more muddled, there is quite a bit of evidence to support the fact that God is more than capable of showing up to people in tangible and personal ways. There is Moses's burning bush, Elijah's chariot, "Behold my Son, in whom I am well pleased,"[1] Saul's road to Damascus, and John's vision on Patmos.

In addition to these, there were the religious relics of the Middle Ages—Jesus' shroud, a sliver from the cross, a shriveled piece of Peter's pancreas—the list goes on and on. Today, every week without exception, there are preachers on my television who declare, "God appeared to me this week and said . . ." They say it *every* week!

In October 1977, forty miles south of Roswell, New Mexico, Maria Rubio found the face of Jesus in a tortilla. Yes, a tortilla. It was in her breakfast skillet, as she prepared a burrito for her husband, Eduardo. The miracle tortilla was later enshrined in a small chapel in Lake Arthur so others could experience Maria's miracle God-sighting as well. Thousands upon thousands have made the tortilla pilgrimage.

In light of these seemingly innumerable God-sightings, it forces me to ponder: *What's the problem with me? What am I doing so wrong?*

These statements may not seem entirely fair. I even concede that they are not fair, but they do illustrate this confusing equation:

All-Powerful + Loving + Apt Communicator = Hidden?

It also speaks to what I too often feel. Throughout history we Jesus-folk have been trying to close the gap between God's revealed abilities and desires and our actual daily experience. The dissonance and disconnect is so strong that we will even believe in a tortilla just to quiet the loneliness.

What are we to do with a God who hides?

You may be one of the lucky few who regularly encounters God in distinct and tangible ways. Based on my experience, you are the exception. The vast majority of the people I meet do not experience God that way. To us, God seems aloof. It is not that God never self-reveals, it is just that those personal appearances are erratic at best, if not all but unheard of.

This perceived aloofness is leading to an unprecedented exodus out of churches. It is having a particularly powerful impact on our children. It is causing famine-faith. And worst of all, it relegates untold numbers to a life of pretending that God is closer than they actually feel him to be, pretending their hearts are spiritually satisfied far more than is true, pretending they are confident when they are stuffing their doubts.

Now, most of you will probably relate to elements of this famine-faith, the kind that longs for God but is left dry ... wanting ... parched. However, if you are among the exceptions, someone who touches God regularly (with your five senses or even your sixth sense), then please read this book anyway. This may give you a window into how the rest of us live and how we strain and squint to believe.

You may already be thinking, *I know exactly what this book is about.* And that may be so. Regardless, I still feel a need to describe the parameters of what we will be discussing in these pages.

First, this book is about tangible encounters with God as a person. I, of course, do not mean God as a human (though God has been known to do that). I mean as *a person*, an actual being with emotions, will, and relationality; one who relates to us. This is in contrast to thinking of God as a breeze or the happy feeling you get on your birthday or as a nondescript burning in your bosom.

I also want to discuss God primarily as a direct communicator. This book does not dispute God's speaking through the Bible and through human history; in fact it assumes God speaks those ways. As for God speaking to us through unexpected people, you may want to read my book *Neighbors and Wise Men: Sacred Encounters in a Portland Pub and Other Unexpected Places.*

Along these same lines, I am not primarily discussing that most significant reality, as my dear friend Richard Twiss used to say, that, "Our problem is not God's absence. It is that God is everywhere at all times. The problem is we are not attuned to his actual ever-presence." My "Uncle" Richard, who died unexpectedly this past year, was an indigenous scholar, a Lakota Sioux, and an amazing follower of Jesus. When he said stuff like this to me, with his long ponytail and green stone earrings dangling from each lobe, it was truly inspiring. And I can't help but believe that he is absolutely right. However, in this book there is something else that I primarily want to explore. I want to reflect on the particular moments of God's uniquely tangible presence and the excruciating pauses in between those rare (and for some, never existent) moments.

Second, this book contains *my* occasional encounters with God, or at least my moments of God's suspicious presence. I say *suspicious* because often it is hard to know for sure if it is God I was sensing after all. I so want to believe that it is God most of the time, that I must confess my capacity to conjure his presence for my own comfort or control. I will try to be honest with you about how convinced I am now whether those few moments were actually God or simply my religious imagination. I will also try to explore the mixed motives that are always present in my religious devotion.

I am aware that I have a real paradox here. I want to discuss my perceptions of God, yet all the while, I must admit that my perceptions are complicated, selfishly fueled, and, at times, dubious.

In this same vein, I have decided not to include certain moments where I am completely incapacitated to evaluate my experience with any objectivity. These moments include my wedding day and the births of my three boys. I am sure God was tangibly present at these events, but I was just too giddy and gooey to notice.

Third, I want to write to you out of my very real (and often quite normal) personal experience. Throughout my life I have witnessed super-Christians. They appear in books or on stages and declare how they seem to have it all figured out, how God shows up for them, and how they experience the supernatural *most of the time*. I am not just talking about TV personalities; I also mean really amazing missionaries and faith-servants from throughout human history. These folks represent a bar of confidence and God-presence that I could never hope to match.

I am not an exceptional spiritual person. I do not have super-faith, like all the missionaries seemed to in my childhood biographies. I am a middle-class guy raised in a midsize town in the Pacific Northwest. I am a lifelong churchgoer and, with admitted struggle and some chapters of spiritual defeat, I have limped along as a follower of Jesus. I love the Trinity, my Bible, and I believe that Jesus Christ is divine and central to the story of the cosmos and the human soul.

Finally, some may assume that this book is attempting to challenge faith or attack God's character. I must assure you that my intention is exactly the opposite.

When I was a boy going to church, I was surrounded by the most lovely, honest, and well-meaning people. One of the things these well-meaning people taught me was that it was not okay to have difficult questions. They didn't do it intentionally or maliciously, but they did it all the same. I was always rewarded when I got an answer correct or responded as a "good" Christian kid should. The few times I attempted to explore a critique or a possible doubt, I was met with a furrowed brow and a correction. I was taught that there was an agreed-upon script and we were not to wander from it.

Those furrowed brows were destructive to an honest faith story. They wounded my soul.

Let's wander from the script, shall we?

I ask you, what greater affirmation of existence is there than talking about a being as if that being is truly there? And I propose that true relationship requires occasional questions, quarrels, rejections, loneliness, appeals, and disappointments. This thought, however, does not erase the joys, hopes, ecstatic moments, quiet comforts, inspirations, and contentments. In real relationships, both exist.

My hope is that you don't primarily look at the pages of this book as you read, but that you personally reflect off of these pages. Prayerfully process God's presence in your own life. After all, why would we expect God to talk to us if we don't have the courage to talk to him? And when talking, to brazenly ask: "God, are you there? Why do you hide from us?"

IN THE BEGINNING

In the beginning . . . God
God was more than singularity
God was more than plurality
God is community
A community of love
God's love is beyond conceiving
Beyond first kiss
Beyond suckling child
Beyond riotous madness
Beyond adrenaline
Beyond erotic intimacy
Beyond free-falling
Beyond intoxication
Beyond self-sacrifice
Beyond . . .

God's communal love could not be contained
Love overflowed
God's cup runneth over

And Creation became
Shinings and shadows became
Deluge and dry-land became
Oaks and olives became
Fire-light and night-lights became
Hummingbirds and hammerheads became
Mice and mammoths became
And finally . . .
God's beloved two-legged masterpieces became

From the Great Artist became artists
And their first words were poetry
"Bone of my bone, flesh of my flesh"
And they all walked together in the cool of the day

The circle of divine love had expanded
But real love requires the right of rejection
In time the two-leggeds rejected
They rejected the circle of love
And they went into hiding

"Where are you?" God said
"We are hiding," the two-leggeds said
Then they lied
Then they blamed
Then they justified
The circle of love had broken
No longer to walk together in the cool of the day
And God let them walk away

Then God went into hiding

Children's Stories by Jonathan Case

PART 1
CHILDREN'S STORIES

WHEN I WAS ONLY, maybe, eight years old, I saw my first movie played on an in-home videocassette recorder (VCR). It was the most unbelievably magical experience. We were just sitting in a normal living room watching on a normal tube television a *real* Hollywood movie. The tape player was the size of a suitcase and must have cost the well-to-do ranch family who owned it thousands of dollars. It had never occurred to me that such a thing was even possible.

The movie was *Superman*, starring Christopher Reeve.

As I sit here now and stretch my memories back to that first VCR encounter, I can still remember the movie through those young eyes. The entire experience was otherworldly . . . and a few particular scenes stuck in my young soul. The first scene was the sight of another child, younger than me, sitting at the bottom of a smokey crater in the middle of a vast Kansas wheat field. The child seemed so small and weak and alone.

The second scene to be lodged in my memory was the sight of that same child lifting up his father's pickup truck.

Children are amazing.

ONE
RANSOM

The pain I feel now is the happiness I had before. That's the deal.

—C. S. LEWIS, *A GRIEF OBSERVED*

"YOUR FOUR-YEAR-OLD CHILD HAS inoperable cancer."

These are words that should never have to be spoken.

In the winter of 2012, my lovely and innocent nephew was diagnosed with a particularly despicable and rare form of liver cancer. The doctors ranted on and on that this obscure type of cancer should never, ever appear in a child. Their defiance was trumped only by their thinly veiled doubt that he would ever be cured. Doubt or not, none of us, neither family nor physicians, were willing to let him die.

This lovely little boy, my nephew: his name is Ransom.

A few months after that fateful diagnosis, my family of five packed our bags and moved from Oregon to Oklahoma to be with my sister, brother-in-law, and their three boys. It was the only response we could come up with. There was nothing in and of ourselves that we could do to heal Ransom. We could not remove the cancer. We could not take away the fear and helplessness. But we could be near. So we moved for the summer, with nothing to offer besides our prayerful presence.

During the moments I was with him, in those early stages of his treatment, Ransom spent much of his time hidden away in his room. Not every stage of his treatment was that way. A young boy's indomitable spirit cannot be contained by sickness. There were many days, maybe most days, when Ransom tore through the chemical fog to run and jump and play with his brothers.

However, on the days that I was with him, particularly those first days, his energy was low. His invasive treatment, delivered though a plastic port in his chest, raged war with his body. His circumstance was inconceivable. To cope, I would have conversations with myself. I would tell myself that it was not really all that bad.

A four-year-old doesn't know any better, right? After all, he is only a child and has never known anything else. To him all this must seem strangely normal. He only knows being tired all the time. He only knows nausea. This terrible existence is, for him, simply "normal." Right?

I wanted to believe it for him. Mostly though, as I think back now, I needed to believe it for myself. It helped me accept the unimaginable.

The first time I really saw him, a couple of days after we arrived in Norman, Oklahoma, I caught him wandering down their hallway. It was a straight corridor from his bedroom to the living space, passing the other boys' rooms, the dining room, and a bath. I stood frozen, maybe forty feet away, watching him. The fingertips of his right hand drug lightly along the textured wall to his right. Just above his outstretched fingers hung pinned-up drawings and art projects, artifacts from a home filled with boyish creativity.

He was almost as bald as me. His face was notably thinner than the last time I had seen him. The skin around his eyes was a bit darker in color.

His steps were tentative. His head hung, bowed ever so slightly. His large bright eyes flashed all around as he crept along. He had the look of a forest animal timidly easing into a clearing.

He wore a worn baby blue T-shirt with the emblem of Batman stretched across his narrow chest. This one single image made me smile inside. I can't completely explain where that smile came from. It may have been the irony. The sight of innocent weakness emblazoned with the symbol of a superhero: fragility and power, sickness and strength, courage and, well, courage. I soon learned that this infirm majesty was the boy's very nature. He was a superhero, and at that moment I decided I would think of him as such from that day forward.

Seconds passed. My little superhero made it to the doorway at that hall's end. He stood there, swaying slightly with his hands extended to the door jam on either side. That was when he heard the sounds. His two older brothers and three cousins, five boys between the ages of five and nine, galloping back and forth across the backyard lawn. He tilted his little bald head, let go with his left hand, and swung like a hinge, his right hand still holding the frame of the doorway. His body tilted away from the doorway until he could see the boys out the wide back window.

The sound of the boys called to him. His muscle memory took over, and he trotted the half a dozen steps to the sliding glass door. He grabbed the handle of the heavy door and leaned as if to pull it open and yet . . . before it budged, he stopped straining and straightened back up. The glass remained still, sealed shut. He gazed at the giggling boys. Another moment passed and then he turned, apparently dismissing the inspiration to join them, and returned back to the almost empty room.

All the while, I had not moved. Just Ransom and me alone in the broad living room.

"Hi Ransom." I leaned to the side and down a bit, hoping to catch his eye.

"Hi." His voice was soft. He didn't look at me.

Instead of the riot in the backyard, he chose the television. Less work.

Ransom used one remote to click on the large flat-screen. Then he grabbed a video-game controller and climbed up into the soft armchair, all but swallowed by the wide pillowed bowl. He was quickly lost in his game. The quiet tapping on the buttons intertwined with his gentle humming as he played.

The game of choice was, of course, superheroes.

I took a seat across from him on the couch. I listened to his humming. Now and again he would talk to himself, or maybe he was talking to me. His thoughts were not profound, just a detail or two about his pixelated companions on the television screen.

This sweet cherub is probably going to die. This thought unexpectedly streaked through my head. It was not something I wanted to think about. Never before had I sat so close to someone so small whose unspoken probability was death.

I wasn't angry, at least not in that moment. I had certainly been angry many times before. God and I had already gone several rounds about Ransom, but not today. My feeling at that moment was sorrow.

What kind of world is this, where four-year-olds suffer and die . . . all pumped full of chemicals . . . weak and sick . . . no desire to eat . . . slowly wasting away and one day . . . gone?

I have always been a person of faith, faltering faith maybe, but faith all the same. I was raised in a Baptist church by devout and hardworking parents. I prayed the salvation prayer when I was a young boy, not much older than Ransom. Church had always been a place of solace throughout my childhood. I was not a particularly smart kid and was painfully awkward. Schoolrooms and ball fields had never been safe places, but Sunday school most always was. It was a place where a kid like me could belong.

I had also never known a time when God-words were not a part of my daily vocabulary. That lifelong habit took over as I watched my nephew play alone.

God, my faith is weak and confused. I want to believe. I want to believe that you are caring for this little boy. I want to believe that you could heal him, but my faith is too weak to ask. I need to believe something.

I paused.

The next thought came clear, so clear it felt like it came from outside me.

God, I want you to show up for this little boy.

I stopped praying.

Is *that* something I can believe? When I say "show up," I don't necessarily mean supernatural healing. I simply wanted to believe that God would be near Ransom. I wanted Ransom to know God's closeness, God's comfort. Whatever time he had left would very likely be full of pain and fear and horrifying confusion. How could a child possibly comprehend . . . this? Even then, my words felt impotent.

I wanted God to be present, even if it was only for moments. I wanted God to be tangible in Ransom's times of terror and unimaginable darkness.

I wanted God to hold his hand.

I wanted God to hold his hand.

———

What are we to do with a God who hides?

My relationship with Ransom, as his uncle and as a human being, has brought this question to violent bearing. It is fresh for me.

I had been told since I was a boy that God loves us. My theological training had taught me that God is a good communicator. God had spoken to the Bible writers. God had appeared to Scripture's holy heroes. God had appeared time and again through the characters of history as my missionary biographies had showed me. And those TV preachers were quick to say that God spoke to them, telling them what to proclaim each week.

Yet God seems silent to me.

Have I just lost the courage to look for God's tangible presence? Can I trust God to show up when I need him?

Can I trust God to show up for Ransom now?

If I hope to answer these questions and more, I fear I need to go back to the beginning. I need to explore the roots of my own beliefs and doubts, and I need to ask, why does God hide from us? And if I dare to be consistent, it is also necessary to ask, why do I hide from God?

TWO
FIRST CONTACT

Father, lay me down to sleep.
I pray the Lord, my soul to keep.
—A CHILD'S PRAYER

MY FIRST ENCOUNTER WITH God happened when I was not much older than Ransom. That feels somehow poetic to me now. It happened in my Grandma's family room one summer afternoon. My parents were off on some vacation, and my sister and I were left in Grandma's care.

You would have loved my grandma.

Grandma was the most honorable of matriarchs. My entire life she has loved our rather large family with integrity and consistency. She has one daughter and four sons, ten grandchildren, and a gaggle of great-grandchildren. Like her pioneer roots, she was hardworking, wise from a life well lived, and not one to waste words. I loved my grandma very much. I miss her. We all do.

In my eyes, as a small boy, my grandma had two great superpowers. I was too young to appreciate her gifts as a schoolteacher or as a loyal churchgoer. My sense of superpowers came from a far different set of values.

Her first power may not seem like much now, but at the time it was nothing less than otherworldly. That supernatural gift: breakfast cereal. Odd, I know, but you see I came from a home strictly defined by "twig and pinecone" breakfast cereals. But not my grandma. After my parents dropped us off at her house and as soon as their car disappeared around the corner, Grandma would gather us into the backseat of her sedan and take us to the largest supermarket in her town. Once we arrived, she would whisk us past the vegetables and wholegrain breads and take us directly to the Emerald City of groceries, the rainbow-colored, sugar-covered land of euphoria. She would stop at the end of the aisle, calmly look down at us, and say, with a whoosh of her hand, "Choose."

I was just learning my letters, but even then I knew that only a place as magical as the cereal aisle could produce fantastical words like *froot* and *puffs*. It would be irreverent to treat such a sanctuary cheaply. My decision could not be made quickly. Every option must be considered. Time was lost in sugar-coated, multi-colored, marshmallow worship. And Grandma? She was content just to watch our lingering decisions of delight.

Eventually we made our selections, be they Smacks, Pebbles, or Krispies, and it was back to Grandma's house for a late morning snack. Within a few days, the boxes would be empty, and we would return to worship once again.

My Grandma had two superpowers. Her other superpower was stories, or to be more accurate, storybooks. She wasn't particularly good at creating stories. I have no idea if she ever wrote stories. She wasn't even much of a storyteller (at least not as I recall). However, she was the family's great dispenser of stories. As a lifelong schoolteacher, my Grandma loved books. And she made sure that my childhood was surrounded by her favorites. Every birthday found new volumes added to my personal library of imagination. Shel Silverstein, A. A. Milne, and Dr. Suess were my grandma's gift of story-guides.

Did I mention that I miss my grandma?

I PRAY THE LORD, MY SOUL TO KEEP.

Grandma's home was an unimpressive ranch house in Newberg, Oregon. It had a style and look appropriate to its time. Entering through the front door, I was met by golds and oranges, bulbous lamps and dark wood-accented furniture. To the left was a hallway to the bedrooms and one bathroom (it contained the toilet that my uncles repeatedly threatened to "flush me down"). To the right were the living spaces: first an open living room, then kitchen, dining room, and family room zigzagging into the house's rear.

My first encounter with God happened on what I remember to be a sunny afternoon. Forgive me, I was very young, so aspects of the memory are even more hazy than most. For instance, I don't remember what day it was. Years later a Sunday school teacher tried to convince me that "it must have been a Sunday." I don't think she could imagine an encounter with God happening on any day other than the "Lord's Day." Out of respect for her station, I chose to believe it was a Sunday. Truth is often sacrificed one small detail at a time.

One thing I can remember for certain was this: I was alone. Alone, that is, except for the ever companionship of grandma's mutt dog, appropriately named Budd. He was ragged and orange, really more Lorax than canine, reasonably friendly, and a good source for childhood entertainment.

I wandered into the family room from the dining room and quietly stood there facing the broad windows, looking out into the backyard. This was the moment when God spoke to me. I offer no greater explanation; I have none. I simply knew it was God. The voice-thought appeared out of nowhere. As near as I can remember, the message was uncomplicated. God plainly said, "It is time."

I knew instinctively what God meant. There was no ceremony. I did not ask for further description. I had no concern for doing it "right" or that screwing it up was even an option. I simply responded.

Next to me was Grandma's tired couch. I knelt down against it and folded my hands on top of the coarse cushions. I closed my eyes. Then I asked Jesus to come into my heart. It only lasted a moment. My prayer may have been no more than a handful of words tossed silently into the sky. It was the business that God had for me. It was brief and intimate, just me, God, and Budd the Lorax-dog.

It may have been my last moment of pure, uncluttered religious freedom.

It was in my Grandma's family room that I came to believe in magic. (Or, if it makes you more comfortable, the "supernatural.")

Writing it now, at forty-two years of age, it seems strange that I was so comfortable with such a magical encounter. It seems odd that I could have such innocent freedom to invite Jesus into one of my organs. But that is just it; it was simple. In fact, it was the most natural thing in the world.

I wish I could return to that sort of simple and exposed freedom. I imagine that this is why Jesus invited us to come as "little children." The decades have added untold layers of ceremonies, critiques, theologies, validations, insecurities, and "maturities" over that once pure surface.

———

Thanks to my Grandma (and others), I was raised on a canon of stories. These stories included wild things and a giving tree. These stories included Luke Skywalker and Prince Caspian. These stories included a floating zoo and a rabbi-healer. Like many children, the manger and the North Pole shared the same breath and the same winter holiday. Aslan and Father Christmas could even be found in the pages of the same formative book about a lion, a witch, and a free-standing upright closet.

The stories of faith and fantasy were so fused that I actually believed that a person could be swallowed by a whale. Seriously. One of these formative story characters performed a great act of disobedience. He ran away from what he knew he must do. He boarded a ship to escape his responsibility. Then, in his darkest moment, he was cast into the sea where he was swallowed by a whale. Yes, a whale! Only then was he fully willing to understand his desire to become a "real boy" . . .

It is odd, isn't it? Can you can see how stories get fused? Pinocchio and Jonah, while it seems confusing now, even amusing, it was not then. It was perfectly natural for a puppet and a prophet to share the same adventure.

These stories were my companions, and they provided me my heroes. So when the magical God told me, "It is time," my response was comfortable and uncluttered. As it should have been. I was a child living in a world of fairy tales. There is nothing wrong with being a child and having a fairy-tale God. Jesus said, "Unless you have the faith of a child, you cannot inherit the kingdom of God."[1] Jesus himself acted like a child in regard to the Father. "The Son can do nothing by himself; he can do only what he sees his Father doing."[2] He was lovely and dependent.

The problem was not the childhood innocence, complete with its fancies and confusions. The problem came in the crushing of those fancies and the innocences they reveal. Once they are gone, what will take their places?

FATHER, LAY ME DOWN TO SLEEP.

I want you to understand something. I truly believed that that first encounter with God was real. Even now, decades later and terribly jaded by life, I still believe that story. It is as real to me as the death of Elvis, which I learned of in Judy Bell's home at age six, or the first space shuttle launch, which I watched from my desk in my fifth-grade classroom. As real as the birth of my little sister, possibly my earliest memory at four years old, or the day I transferred schools in the middle of first grade, fearfully far from my friends. That afternoon in Grandma's family room is simply history, both then and now.

So, a few years later, when one of my Sunday school teachers asked me about my "conversion," I spoke to her with freedom and ease. I was happy that she was so interested in me. It was fun for me to tell her my story . . . but that sense of freedom and fun did not last.

I was about nine years old.

"Tony, have you asked Jesus to be your Lord and Savior?" she asked. She was a lovely and kind woman, the sort of lifelong servant that every church depends upon.

"Yes," I quickly answered. A smile grew across her face, and I was glad that I had answered her question correctly.

"That makes me very happy," she said. "Can you tell me about it? How did it happen? Did it happen at church camp?"

"*Umm*, no. It didn't happen at camp." I wanted to tell her about my grandma's house, but instead of letting me just talk, she jumped to her next question.

"Did it happen at church?" Her smile shrank with each question.

"No, it didn't happen at church," my voice was becoming unsettled. I was hoping that her smile would return.

"Okay then, let's try this another way. Tony, *who* was with you when you prayed to ask Jesus into your heart?"

Oh boy. I did not like where this was going at all. I stared at her blankly. As you can guess, this did not provide any comfort to my Sunday school teacher. I honestly didn't know how to answer. I was quite sure that "my grandmother's orange dog" was not the answer she was looking for.

"Tony. Who was with you? It is a simple question. Who *led* you to Jesus?" I'm sure she was trying to be helpful. "It is a simple question that everyone should be able to answer. Who was with you?"

My confusion now turned to fear. I didn't want to upset her. I also knew I wasn't supposed to lie. So I just stared, my mouth hanging open.

"Was it your mommy? Was your mommy with you?"

"No," my voice now sheepish. I could no longer look at her face.

"Was it your daddy?"

"No." *No* had become a three-syllable word as it stumbled over my tongue.

"It must have been somebody. It is okay, Tony, just tell me who it was. Was it a pastor or another Sunday school teacher . . . or a friend, maybe?"

I couldn't answer anymore. There was this terrible look in her eyes. It was probably just the look of confusion, but it felt like disappointment. I was engulfed by the feeling that I had done something wrong.

It didn't take much longer for the conversation to come to an end and for my teacher to shoo me back to the day's activities. I joined in with the other kids. On the outside, I may have appeared unfazed, but inside, my doubts feasted.

That night, more than an hour after bedtime, this small and insecure boy lay awake, unable to sleep, oppressed by his memories of the day.

What did I do wrong? I asked myself. *I didn't know that you aren't allowed to be alone. Will I get a second chance to do it right? How on earth could I have messed this up so bad?* Thinking back now, it seems like an overreaction, to say the least, but I can't deny the memory. Then the most chilling thought of all, for a religious child like me, crashed into my mind. *Does this mean I am going to hell?*

There it was, the granddaddy of all questions. It looped around and around in my head like a carrousel. *Am I going to hell? Am I going to hell? Am I going to hell?* I thought of nothing else. And the fear stole my sleep.

Why do we do this to our children? I am sure that we most often do it unknowingly, as most likely was the case with my Sunday school teacher. But we need to remember that children have a theology too.

It may seem clumsy or rudimentary, but it is a theology. The difference between a child and an adult is not primarily the content of the theology. The biggest difference is the impact of that theology.

As adults we are able to compartmentalize our religious thoughts. For instance, many religious adults believe that a portion of humanity is heading toward hell and that hell is a very scary place, yet they still manage to walk blithely through a supermarket, sit casually in a board meeting, or attend a sporting event without freaking out at the inevitable carnage that swirls all around them.

Children are different. They actually believe their beliefs and that those beliefs have present consequences. When I was nine, the concept of hell really scared me. It scared me with the same intensity that my first encounter with God had put my heart at peace.

———

Am I going to hell?

After laying wide awake for what felt like hours, my mind came to terms with the question. I managed to do enough theological gymnastics (as much as a nine-year-old can) to allow me to calm my soul, alleviate my fear, and, at last, fall asleep. But before I finally nodded off, I took the lessons from that day to heart:

1. Encounters with God should be treated with suspicion.
2. Be very careful when admitting any strange events involving God.
3. Learn the accepted ways of talking about God, and stick to those approved scripts.
4. If I want to avoid this mistake in the future, I must learn from the religious people around me. They will teach me how to believe and how to talk about God.

What else was a boy to do? What else is any of us to do?

THREE
GOD GAMES

This little light of mine, I'm gonna let it shine.
Won't let Satan poof it out, I'm gonna let it shine.
—A SUNDAY SCHOOL SONG

AFTER THE CONVERSATION WITH my Sunday school teacher, God pretty much went into hiding. I don't know if the hiding was God's decision or mine, though I was pretty sure that I had done something to mess everything up.

I think it is difficult for most of us to express ourselves when it comes to our actual lives with God.

Most of the people I know, even the very religiously oriented people, don't really talk like they encounter God in direct and tangible ways. For the most part, we talk *about* God. Our conversations are full of the ideas of God. When I listen to people talk, including myself, I often find myself wondering if we even believe that God is a *person*. You know, *a person*: a dynamic and living being with thoughts, emotions, intents, and actions. Most people speak as if God is just an *ideology*: a set of concepts, arguments, guidelines, and categories.

God is presented as something that people need to be convinced of, as opposed to someone they can be introduced to.

God is something that needs to be explained, as opposed to someone to be encountered.

God is something to be understood, as opposed to someone to be known.

How do we harmonize with a God whom we experience as tangibly distant but believe to be personally involved?

———

As a boy, I believed I was the only person on earth.

I feel like a crazy person writing these words now. However, it was one of the games that I would play in my mind to try to bring narrative to the faith I was taught to believe versus the actual world that I lived in every day.

Since God was not tangible, I needed to have a framework for how God was actively involved in my story. The "only person on earth" conclusion was no doubt fueled by a child's narcissism, but I think that is somewhat reasonable. After all, what does a child know? A child cannot conceive of another person's mind or experience. They cannot imagine the world in any abstraction apart from their daily experience. As a result, Little Tony had to find a conceivable reduction.

A conceivable reduction, no matter how fanciful, is often more bearable to the soul than a hopeless dissonance.

My particular reduction was a game. I am not sure what else to call it. It was an epic game that was as wide as the world and as serious as death. The game had two teams, God and Satan. *I* was the field of battle. It was a game about life. My life. This game about me had only one purpose (the only purpose my religious training cared about): to save my soul.

You may be asking yourself, "What about all the other people?" If *I* was the field of battle and the game was about my life, what about my parents' lives? What about my schoolmates or all the folks in my childhood church? What about the billions of people across the globe, assuming they actually exist? Well, for the game to work, their presence was pragmatic and perfunctory. They played a role in the game, but they were not the purpose of the game.

Now, I did spend quite a bit of time thinking about all these other people and the quality of their existence. I wanted their lives to matter as well. The answer I came up with was theological; it required the concept of eternity. Time is limitless. In the classroom, I was taught that there was more than enough time for an amoeba to turn into Michael Jordan, so it is logically consistent to believe that there was plenty of time for everyone to get their chance to play the God-game.

And get their chance they would, but not now. This life, the life I was living, was only about me. The others would have to wait their turn.

There were other implications to my cosmic game. For instance, China did not exist. Lots of places did not exist. Why would they need to exist? I was not there. They didn't affect me or my story. Now, should a place like China need to exist, for example, because I was watching a news story on television, God had that handled. He would quickly build a China set and fill the set with China-looking people. This seemed to me much more convenient for God. Why keep China open all the time when it was only needed for a thirty-second news segment?

So the game went something like this (as I said before, there were two players—one was God, who I knew was the good guy, and the other was Satan): The battle was for my eternal salvation or flesh-eating damnation (my Uncle Jim had taught me that hell was like an ever-burning fireplace where the pain never stopped and the flames never cooled). It was not a game to be trifled with. The stakes were high, as high as they come.

In my imagination, these two combatants sat at a giant stone table. The surroundings were a cross between Dungeons and Dragons, Narnia, and Dante's Inferno. God sat on one side, all misty and translucent. Through his mistiness, God looked like He-Man, the muscle-bound, blond and bronze, fantasy action-hero of my youth ... only, well, God and old. He-Man's archenemy was called Skeletor, a demonic man-beast dressed in black and blue leather and a hideous grinning skull for a head. Satan looked like that, only uglier ... and meaner ... and, well, covered in flames. They sat together—God, all Shechinah and surrounded by harp music; Satan with toxic breath and the muffled sound of tortured screaming oozing from beneath his heavy metal cloak. There was no need for pleasantries or pretext. They had come to negotiate the terms of the game, which effectively defined the parameters of my life. Then, based on these negotiated parameters, we would discover: What will Little Tony choose? Will he choose heaven, or will he choose hell?

The negotiation went something like this, as my child-brain conceived it.

God started in a voice like Charlton Heston: "You cannot have his family. They are mine. His parents will be Christians, and they will go to church." (Little Tony could not imagine a God who did not place this as the highest priority.)

> Satan: "Curses! Okay, since you are the Master of the
> Universe, I will give you that one, but ... *umm*, in
> return, Tony will be raised in a secular culture full of
> drugs, rock 'n' roll music, and TV shows like *Three's
> Company*." (My dad always hated that show.)
> God: "You're a mean one, Mr. Satan. Okay, next he will get
> to attend a good Baptist church."
> Satan: "Not a perfect church."
> God: "Well, no, it will not be a perfect church"—both
> God and Satan sort of chuckled just a moment at that
> thought, then God continued—"Let's say, his church
> will be a B-plus."
> Satan: "C-plus."

God: "Okay, a B, but don't push me."

Satan: "Fine, fine. He can have your precious church on Sundays and even Wednesday nights, but five days a week he will be sentenced to—(dramatic pause)—the public school system! (Menacing chuckle) It will be full of secular books, evolution, and . . . wait for it . . . sex education! BruuHahahahahaha."

In my overly stimulated imagination, fueled by ample amounts of TaB, it would go on like this for a while. God would demand Christian musicians like Amy Grant and Keith Green, and Satan would counter with AC/DC and Queen (complete with backmasking the secret message "It's fun to smoke marijuana" behind the hit song "Another One Bites the Dust"). God would get church camp, and in exchange Satan would get drugs and pornography. God wanted to include Billy Graham and Ronald Reagan, and Satan would balance with Shirley McClain and John Denver. (What can I say, Baptists were really worried about the "New Age" back then.)

As a result, my life was the playing out of the salvation possibilities within these predetermined variables. God had carefully, and I believed lovingly, set these parameters in place. There was plenty to test the quality of my moral and spiritual resolve, while maintaining more than enough to help me find God's "narrow way."

Now, which path would I choose?

Today, as I think back, I am amazed by the theological sophistication of a child's imagination. Think about it. I had created a game that allowed God to be instrumental in my life without being actually involved. It was the stuff of a personalized deism. God was personal and even concerned, but also distant and emotionally obtuse. I think many of us live our lives this way, minus the Saturday-morning-cartoon flourishes.

Deism is a belief system where one believes in God, or at least a divine of some kind, but this divine is wholly separate from the actual ongoing events of this world. Some refer to this as the Clockmaker Theory, where God initially created the "clock" of the universe, wound this "clock" up, and then stepped away and let the springs and gears of his creation run their course. In other words, God is inaccessibly distant. As a boy, I was not educated enough to understand the Clockmaker theology, but I was imaginative enough to create a scenario that made sense to me. It may seem silly to you, but it certainly made more sense than the belief that "God speaks to us all the time, if only we would just listen." I had listened, and God was not talking.

So why am I spending so much time tinkering with the imaginations of a religiously obsessed child? Certainly it may give me some hints into what Ransom is experiencing. I wonder what sort of game Ransom thinks God is playing. I wonder what sort of priorities he believes God might have. When God sat at the stone negotiating table of Ransom's life, what did God get in exchange for cancer? I wonder how Ransom might conceive of spiritual fairness, like when his brothers and cousins are giggling on the trampoline outside his window. The odd thing is, I may be very surprised by *his* imaginations. He may have a sort of peace and clarity I cannot comprehend. He may very well have something to teach a weathered cynic like me.

As significant as it is to try to understand Ransom (as well as my three young boys and millions of other children), processing these memories are also important to understanding the adult who stares back at me from my bathroom mirror. I don't know that any of us can understand where we are and why we believe unless we examine the lower strata of our spiritual sediment.

It is difficult to understand what we have become unless we understand *from where* we have come.

Those early beliefs, even the very first beliefs we had as children, no matter how fanciful, could offer a key to understanding our inner lives today. Was everybody else taught to ignore those early imaginations the way that I was? Maybe it is time to do some personal excavating. What are your formative childhood memories about God? Why do you think those particular memories have stuck with you versus the millions of memories that time has lost?

I am coming to believe that our adult faith is often just a more refined and justifiable version of those early childhood themes. Do I still believe that life with God is a cosmic game? Do I still believe that God sits at a stone table and that Satan is dressed like the lead singer of the rock band KISS? Of course not. However, if I am brutally honest, I often treat it like a game all the same.

GOD GAME BELIEFS

BELIEF: IT IS A GAME

Don't we often see this world as God's chessboard? We betray that belief every time we cheer for our political party's victory as if it is a glorious move by God to advance our "white" pieces on the game board. And when the "wrong" piece of legislation passes, do we mourn as if God's strategic position has been weakened?

On the Bible-college basketball court, when a guy makes his free throws, we say, "You must have said your prayers this morning." It is supposed to be funny, but it also betrays a subtle form of religious fatalism.

Do we treat God's blessings as a game to be manipulated?

"If I just give 10 percent to my church, then God might change my financial picture."

"If I just get up early and read my Bible every morning, then God will . . ."

"If I just give up my favorite vice, maybe God will give me . . ."

Isn't it all strategic negotiation?

There are subtle but insidious ways that this game paradigm causes us to choose teams like children on the schoolyard. It is essential that my team "win," often with little regard for the other team's eternal destiny. I want me and my team to win so badly that I will even cook the books of belief. For instance, I will ignore large swaths of the Bible that don't make a case for my team's particularities. I will fall back on a charismatic teacher for psychological assurance. I will use absolutism (and ignore mystery and paradox) so that my beliefs are mathematically right, thus insuring that my team wins.

I fear that I still believe much like a game, and I imagine that my lifetime of steeping in Western competitiveness and pragmatism hasn't helped.

BELIEF: FUNCTIONAL DEISM

All of these games and all of this self-obsession are just some of the techniques I have perfected to keep (or cope with) God at a distance. If I treat God as a series of negotiated parameters as opposed to an interacting presence, it would help explain why faith feels the way it does. In a weird way, it actually helps.

For instance, what are we to do with the belief that "God is good all the time" and yet emotionally cope with a world filled with annihilating tsunamis, planes that fly into skyscrapers, and cancer? One of the most popular mechanisms is functional deism. To cope, we assert that God is simply *not* actively involved in these awful things. God cannot be blamed. Then it is a natural step to apply that same logic to all of life: God is simply not involved.

On a practical level, every time we place our trust in our own efforts to care for our families, we are functional deists. Any time our hope is in our skills, shrewd contacts, or bank accounts to provide, instead of believing in the feeder of sparrows and the clothier of lilies (Matthew 6), we are functional deists. When we shape our faith primarily based on a collection of right ideas and approved behaviors as opposed to an abiding presence (John 15), we are functional deists.

Once you start thinking about it, the list goes on and on. What would you add?

BELIEF: THE GAME IS ALL ABOUT ME

As much as it is embarrassing to admit what a self-addicted narcissist I was as a child, the truth is I don't know that things have changed very much. When I pray for God's presence, I rarely think about the implications it would have on anybody else. I pray, "God please give me that job," without any consideration for the dozen people who would, therefore, not get the job.

Also, there is my ever-obsession with seeing the ways of God in terms of people just like me (look like me, spend like me, think like me, read like me, vote like me, etc.). My religious beliefs seem to benefit people like me, no matter how much interpretive gymnastics those beliefs require. For example, I simply dismiss the possibility that Jesus' words to the Rich Young Ruler in Mark 10 directly apply to me, even though, based on sheer volume of wealth, I may be many times more wealthy than he was. I guess that the Rich Young Ruler probably had a very small home (by our standards), with few "luxuries" (like plumbing, heat, or electricity), and he probably had a small closet of outfits and a small handful of shoes. For these things he was considered "rich." Despite my comparative wealth (and embarrassing number of shoes), I still contend that Jesus' words to that young rich man do not apply to someone like me. There is no way that the Messiah would critique middle-class America in that way.

When we pray to win the lottery, do we ever consider the untold numbers who would therefore not win? Do we think about all those other folks, many of whom are in dire straits, unemployed, maybe with hungry kids? Do our prayers naturally drift to other people for whom a winning ticket would be a way out of poverty, abuse, or oppression? I am not just talking about a literal lottery here, since so many of our prayers are an appeal for luck.

When we pray for our kids to make the basketball team or be accepted to a certain college, do we ever think of the other kids who will be left out if God fulfills our prayers?

How about when we pray for our church to grow? Do our prayers, be they private or from the pulpit, include remorse and regret for all the small churches that will need to close their doors to make way for another urban megachurch? The statistics are indisputable: churches grow because other churches shrink or close. Do our prayers include them?

My prayers are dominated by me and *my* people. Do I pray for other countries to succeed or just my country? Do I take into compassionate consideration that many, many other countries are filled with poverty, famine, and epidemics that would make our poorest neighborhoods look like paradise? Do we pray for the success of our neighbors across the globe?

How about when we pray for our soldiers? Do our appeals drift to the soldiers on the other side, for their safety and spared life? How about their families?

In the end, I believe that most of us are narcissists when it comes to our God-imaginations. God is at the game table, and we believe he should be skewing the game to support me, my people, my church, my country, my . . . my . . . my . . .

Am I the only one treating it all like a game?

FOUR
SUPERHERO SERUM

My God is so great, so strong and so mighty,
there's nothing my God cannot do.
—A SUNDAY SCHOOL SONG

FAITH SEEMS TO COME so easy to some people.

By the time I was a young teenager, I found myself looking around my church youth group and seeing a selection of kids who just seemed to get it. There was a certain magic to their faith. They were baffling to me. I had no such magic.

The magic looked like this: There was a tall and proper young lady who never seemed to have a hair out of place. She walked with the very blessings and grace of heaven. There was Strong Jock, all charismatic and complete. He was quickly given the microphone and always had the right answer, full of courage and confidence. There was Bryan the Evangelist, known for always bringing the "lost kids" with him to church. One Sunday he arrived with his school's entire soccer team.

And then there was me. No magic. No superpower. I had a hole in the middle of my chest. It was an infected hole, full of doubt, confusion, and cowardice. What was it about these special few, these Sunday morning superstars? Why was my life with God so clumsy?

As I sit here writing, my nine-year-old is sitting next to me. He is carefully drawing superheroes. I used to love to draw superheroes. When I was nine, the only thing I wanted for my birthday was a book called *How to Draw Comics*. I meditated on its pages. It taught me how to carefully craft superheroes of my own, magical warriors with any powers I could dream up. Some would have super strength and others could fly, but all were endowed with courage, goodness, and confidence. Because of my fascination, I always assumed that I would be a comic artist someday. And then I learned that those jobs require a certain artistic aptitude. Oh well.

How does one become a superhero? So many superheroes started out no more impressive than me. This was very reassuring to a kid who spent most of his high school years in the shadows. I didn't even sniff puberty until my junior year. My awkwardness was contained in a five-foot-two frame carrying an imposing one hundred pounds. Peter Parker, who later became Spider-Man, seemed as scrawny and clumsy as I felt. Bruce Banner, who later became the muscle-bound Incredible Hulk, was socially awkward and unimpressive. Even Clark Kent, alter ego to Superman, seemed to trip over his own feet and say the wrong things more often than not. But what made these people special? What made them heroes? They had stumbled upon the magic. You know what I mean? They had discovered a transformative magic, and it had set them free. Peter Parker was bitten by a radioactive spider; Bruce Banner was hit with a bolt of gamma rays; Clark Kent was empowered by our yellow sun. And *blam!*, these seemingly normal guys were transformed. This transformation left them no longer simple and marginalized; they were now "amazing," "incredible," and "super."

As a boy and into my teens, I was always looking for that missing magic in my faith life. I wanted the super-faith serum, whatever it might be. I was sure it must be out there somewhere. There were those around me, few though they may be, who had obviously found it. They had the magic that I lacked. They spoke about God from a place of courage and assurance. They acted like God spoke to them, and I wanted that. I wanted that more than anything else in the world.

I can remember sitting in church one Sunday morning. I could not have been older than twelve or thirteen. My pastor, wise and tall, was standing behind the wide lectern, as imposing as a tower on a castle wall. Behind him was the cascading choir loft and cross, reaching to the rafters. To his right and his left stood the American flag and the Christian flag, equal in size and prominence. I sat in the balcony. I was in the front row and center, across from the preacher, ground zero for his inspiring sermon. Our old Baptist church was built with a wraparound balcony, and though the space could hold many hundreds of people, you always felt close to the stage. I leaned forward, over the railing, as he spoke. I felt like I was floating over the congregation below.

"Do you want to supercharge your Christian life?" He was coming to the end of his stirring sermon. It was time to not just inspire but to give his congregation the exhortation of the week.

Inside, I wanted to cry out, "Yes! Yes, I want a supercharged Christian life. Supercharge me, Pastor! Supercharge me!"

"If you want to supercharge your Christian life, there is one thing that every Christian can do." At that moment, he had me. No matter what he said, I was ready to do it. "Go home and set your alarm clock one half hour earlier, and start each day reading the Word of God."

Set your alarm clock? Really? I thought. *No magical prayer? No secret formula? This seems a bit suspicious . . .*

"I promise you," my pastor continued, "there is no greater remedy for our spiritual weaknesses than starting the day reading the Bible. If you commit your day to God, he will commit himself to you."

What can I say? He is the pastor and he knows best.

I was only a boy at the time. I can clearly remember the emptiness and confusion I felt about my spiritual state. Throughout my young life, I had tried, falteringly tried, to do everything I had been told by pastors, Sunday school teachers, and camp counselors, yet still my insides felt all wrong. I was sure that there was something that I had missed. That morning, I believed that my pastor had seen the gaping doubt in the middle of my chest and he had brought me some magic. It was an odd sort of magic, but I believed it was magic all the same. I still remember the relief and resolve that I felt.

On the way home from church, I climbed out of my captain's chair in the back of our custom Chevy van (back in the day when our lap belts were still considered "optional"), and I kneeled between my parents' seats and asked them if I could please have an alarm clock.

Back home they found a radio clock, and I situated it next to my bed. I set that alarm for six-thirty and for the next few years, I awoke every morning and read a few chapters of my Bible. Often, maybe even usually, I felt like I was just running my eyes over the words, but I read every day all the same. I was waiting for the supercharge that my pastor had promised. I am ashamed to confess: the magic never came.

Even so, I continued my quest for the spiritual secret I lacked. My youth pastor, Rudy, and I had many discussions on the topic. I had no doubt about his desire to help, but none of the mottos or formulas seemed to work on me.

Me? Maybe *that* was the problem: me. I was the problem. Maybe I was just broken.

By the time I was sixteen years old, I still felt terribly distant from God. Keith Green, an early Christian folk singer, had a song that went like this:

> *My eyes are dry*
> *My faith is old*
> *My heart is hard*
> *My prayers are cold*
> *And I know what I ought to be*
> *Alive to You and dead to me.*

I know I was just a boy and regrettably serious about such things, but what else was I to do? That is what my faith felt like, and my doubts were starting to outgrow my confidences. What do I mean by *doubt*? To be honest with you, my doubts were not about the content of Christian faith. Sure I had some questions (questions I felt like I had to keep hidden or risk rejection). In my child's mind, I questioned things like: If salvation is based on God sacrificing his Son, what's the sacrifice? God knows everything, so he knew he would get Jesus back after just three days in the ground. That doesn't seem like much of a sacrifice (three days for an eternal being). But these were confusions more than doubts. I believed in Jesus, that he had walked on the earth, did miracles, gave beautiful teachings, and eventually died on a cross for the sins of the world. I believed the Bible. I even believed the awkward teachings about the Trinity, though I found the three-in-one/one-in-three explanations based on water (ice, water, steam) or an egg (shell, white, yoke) to be less than intellectually satisfying. *Really, God is an unfertilized chicken fetus?* If they had just kept the explanation as, "God is ultimately too complicated and wonderful for us to get our tiny brains around," I think that would have been more spiritually and intellectually satisfying than "God is an egg."

My doubt was not primarily about ideas. It was this: I doubted that the system worked at all. From the pulpit, at the conferences, and on the television, the language was so triumphal. "Believe this and your life will be full of peace, hope, joy, and purpose. Just trust God and he will do the rest." I didn't believe these preachers anymore. I had witnessed the flash of white-hot anger when the pastor yelled at kids running through the hallways of our church. I also sensed these leaders' unspoken doubts.

I certainly knew those doubts in me. I doubted that God could be near. I doubted that I could feel spiritually alive (have peace, hope, joy, purpose.) As the years went on, I feared that my faith was on a self-destructive course.

In my sixteenth year, I decided I was done with half measures.

Getting an alarm clock and volunteering to teach Vacation Bible School were not doing the job. I needed something more . . . something dramatic.

The greatest act of faith-devotion I could think of was to become a missionary. What else is there? It was the one thing I had feared all my life. *Please God, please, please, please don't make me a missionary. Please don't send me to Africa,* had been among my lifelong prayers. But like I said, the time for half measures was over. It was time to push through my fear.

So, I decided to be a missionary. It was only for a summer, but it felt like so much more. It was a fork in the road. A road diverged in a wood, and I, I took . . . the narrow way.

My parents reluctantly but graciously gave me their permission. I applied to a missionary agency and raised my own funds (mostly from church friends). And the summer of my sixteenth year, I climbed on a cross-continental bus for six days, then a plane and another plane and one last bus, to finally arrive at an orphanage in Ecuador.

At first, it was all that I hoped it would be, just like the black-and-white photos in the back of my missionary biographies. The orphanage was built on a hillside, a terraced Crayola box of gardens, playful children, and exotic animals.

I joined a team of missionary teens and adults.

I knew that the secret I had been looking for must be here; I only had to find it. Where was God? Was God in the faces of these giggling orphans? Was God in the lambs born my first week on site? Was God in the panoramic valley laid out beneath my dormitory door? Was God in the sweat and calluses from long days of construction? Was God in the faces of Indian children who watched our gospel puppet shows? If God was there, I could not see him. I did not know how to see him.

I clung to those black-and-white missionary photos in my memory, which I knew proved the magic. My unspoken gamble was this: if I could not find the magic here, then my journey with God was done. If not here, then there were only two options, both unthinkable. Either the problem was with me—I am simply broken, thus there is no reason to continue to believe—or the other more terrifying option: the entire Christian system is broken. And if that is true then we are all screwed.

You can probably guess what happened.

God didn't show. As far as I could discern, God made no attempt to reciprocate my grandiose act of faith. None.

God was too busy to bother with me, and his human representatives offered little help. The adult leaders painfully let me down. I am sure that I was judging them based on an impossible standard. But screw that. This was my life and my hope. I had come to the end of my young religious rope. I idolized those leaders. They were real missionaries, and yet, what did I witness? More of the same. Their words were just as triumphal as what I had heard all my life, only their lives stood in even greater tragic contrast. They were petty and angry with rarely a word of regret, confession, or apology. As a result, the hole in my chest continued to fester.

I was not, however, going down without a fight. I chose to dare the fates (and God if he was listening). I started to express my discontent. I brought some of my long-held doubts into the light. However, those admissions met disapproving looks of religious disappointment. It seemed that the more I faith leapt, the more the heavens remained cold and silent and that hole in my chest began to stink.

I had given all I knew how to give, and the result was the same. If the magic was out there, it was clearly not available to me.

On the long flight home from Ecuador, I sorrowfully surrendered to what felt like my only option. There were no more risks for me to take. I was simply broken. I concluded that the God who seems to speak so readily to others simply does not speak to me. So my life with God was over.

———

Faith-life certainly does not end at sixteen. Our human programming will not allow it. There is something in all of us that longs for God. Even the atheist seems to evidence that reality when he rails against God's existence with scorned veracity. How can one be scorned by something that is not there?

My driving desire was not to be the smartest Christian (at least not most of the time), or the most holy Christian (a lost cause for sure), or even to have other people compliment my faith. At my deepest level, I wanted to believe that it worked, simply worked. I wanted to know that God was real and that I had not done something to irrevocably disqualify myself from the God-life.

Over the decades to come, I found myself returning time and again to the quest for "missing magic." I wanted my spiritual life to be special and for God to be near. There were times when I begged spiritual folk around me to pray that I might receive an additional "blessing" on my life. Those prayers never seemed to work on me like they worked on others. In my midtwenties, I fasted for forty days, hoping that it would take my God-life to a new level. Many times over the years, I escaped to mountain monasteries to pray with monks that I might be whole and new. There were these examples and a hundred other attempts to find the magical elixir, the secret spell, or the superhero serum.

Why do we do this? Why do we switch churches looking for something new? Why do we surrender ourselves to the new charismatic preacher with the absolutist answers? Why do we "go ancient"? Why do we trust the "five steps to purpose" or the magical prayer of a long-dead saint? Why do we think, *If I could just get more passionate about my moral/political beliefs,* or *If I could just have the courage to carry a picket sign,* or *What if I share a gospel tract?*

On some level, isn't much of religion a quest for the missing? If only I could find that allusive *something,* maybe God would finally appear.

We see this search for the magic-something in folks like Simon in Acts: "When Simon saw that the Spirit was bestowed through the laying on of the apostles' hands, he offered them money, saying, 'Give this authority to me as well, so that everyone on whom I lay my hands may receive the Holy Spirit.' But Peter said to him, 'May your silver perish with you, because you thought you could obtain the gift of God with money!'"[1] Or the rich lawyer who came to Jesus and asked, "Teacher, what good thing shall I do that I may obtain eternal life?"[2] And maybe I am like the young lawyer. I feel like I am asking the question with virtuous humility, but in truth I am not able or programmed to accept the answer that Jesus gives.

Maybe this search for magic is why Jesus said such things as:

Not everyone who says to Me, "Lord, Lord," will enter the kingdom of heaven, but he who does the will of My Father who is in heaven will enter. Many will say to Me on that day, "Lord, Lord, did we not prophesy in Your name, and in Your name cast out demons, and in Your name perform many miracles?" And then I will declare to them, "I never knew you; depart from Me."[3]

Magic may not be the secret after all.

FIVE
MAKE BELIEVE

Maybe there's a God above
But all I've ever learned from love
Was how to shoot at someone who outdrew you
It's not a cry you can hear at night
It's not somebody who has seen the light
It's a cold and it's a broken Hallelujah
—LEONARD COHEN

I WISH THAT I could say that the plane flight home from Ecuador was the end of my childhood faith story, but there is one more nail to drive into my faith coffin. It is an important story because it illustrates one more layer of faith-death and God-silence.

Upon my return home, I received a phone call from one of my pastors. Ours was a large church, and I was very surprised that one of these superstar pastors would even know who I was, let alone call me at home.

My mom called me from the kitchen of our University District home. I had returned only a few days before, and I was basking in the comfort of my Mom's effusive attention. I picked up the receiver, which she had laid on the countertop. I stretched the springy cord out into the dining room so I could sit on a cushioned window seat, my back against the leaded-glass windows.

"Tony, I just called to say welcome home. We are all so proud of you, and we are so thankful for your safe return. Praise the Lord. How was your mission?"

I really had no idea how to answer his question. I was pretty sure that "I have decided not to be a Christian" would not be received well. The line sat silent for a few seconds, and then I started my response with, "Good, I guess . . . it was—"

"That's great," he quickly jumped in. "We are so happy that you are home, and we want to give you a chance to share this Sunday at church before the entire congregation. Could you please come to the church around eight a.m. and we will get you all set up? Once again, welcome home. Can't wait to hear about your trip."

And with that, there was a click on the other end.

Oh, crap.

Sunday arrived.

I stood just offstage on the slowly circling stairwell, with entrances climbing from the sanctuary up to the stage, then the choir loft, and eventually into the baptismal hidden high behind the sliding paneled back wall. The service began with praise anthems from the full choir loft, a musical wave of red robes.

I peeked out the cracked door. Our church was fairly formal back then, most everyone in suits or dresses. It had never been an option for me to attend Sunday service in anything less than a nice collared shirt. The lower level was almost full, and the balcony had begun to fill as well. It was a lovely sanctuary with a classic stage, chandeliers, and ornamental moldings throughout.

What have I gotten myself into? I thought. I was in a real pickle. *There must be a million people out there.* In truth, it was far less than a thousand, but that didn't matter. It was not about the numbers anyway; those seats were full of people I had known all my life. Many of those very people had given money to pay for my mission. I knew that they wanted to know that their money went to good use. Also my parents and my pastors were there, people whose approval held the keys to my self-esteem. And finally, most every Sunday school teacher I had ever had was in attendance, these loving saints who had innocently and unintentionally taught me to hide my doubts and only answer questions according to the approved party line.

When the final chord from the pipe organ dissipated, the pastor asked the choir and the congregation to sit down. He gave a few announcements and then invited me to join him out on stage. I took a deep breath and slowly opened the side door and began the long walk to the platform's center. I was wearing my best clothes and tried to walk as tall as my unimpressive frame could muster. "We have a real treat," he said, "one of our young people has just gotten home from a great missionary adventure. He wanted to come out here and tell you all about his time in South America and to give testimony to what the Lord has done. Tony, tell us about your trip." Then he handed me the microphone and fixed his smile on me.

I gripped the microphone in my sweaty hand and hid my face behind the baseball-sized black foam cover. I stared around the room, first across the balcony peopled with silhouettes before the sun-filled windows, then across the main floor where the church's aristocracy sat, including my parents in their usual seat: fourth row on the left side.

What was I to do? What else could I do? From my earliest days in this building, I had learned how to behave: to sit in the front row, to memorize Bible verses every week, and to raise my hand first when any Bible question was asked. I knew my role, and this morning was no different. Submissively, I played that role the only way I knew how. I stood there and gave the *right* answers. In other words, I lied. That's right, I lied. I lied and I lied, then I lied some more. I talked about how amazing the trip had been. I told them that I had never felt God was so near. I told them I had been changed forever. I told them that I was sure and thankful for my faith.

And as those polluted words flowed out from my soul, in behind them washed a tide of shame. What kind of person could stand on *that* stage, in front of *those* holy people, under that cross . . . and lie?

What the heck was wrong with me? What sort of hell was inside of me?

———

Why do we use our children to justify our beliefs? I wonder if part of it is because deep down inside, we don't really believe. Maybe we need our children to provide the evidence that at least the system works for someone, particularly the "innocent." It is much the same way we use our pastors; we lean so heavily on their confidence, because deep down our hope is actually thin. As long as that smart preacher up there believes this stuff, I have greater confidence that our shared beliefs are true. I need someone else's faith to lean on.

Be it pastor or child, I fear it is little more than vicarious faith.

I had come to the end. My inner concoction was a mixture of failure, shame, doubts, and mere exhaustion from trying so long. Whatever it was, I quit. It was my senior year. I figured I could endure the religious pageantry for another nine months. No one needed to know. I certainly didn't want to drag any of my friends into my pit of doubt. I also knew that I didn't want to hurt my mom.

It was the end of my childhood and ironically, the death of my faith as well.

He wanted to care, and he could not care. For he had gone away and he could never go back anymore. The gates were closed, the sun was down, and there was no beauty left.

—F. SCOTT FITZGERALD

So I pretended for that one last year. It was "make believe" (a surprisingly ironic idiom.) And I discovered that pretending was not that hard. Church was my culture, as comfortable to me as being an Oregonian. The culture of Christianity came naturally to me.

I learned that pretending can be comfortable, very comfortable. Everyone around me was perfectly unfazed with my pretending. I think they preferred it. I discovered that religion encourages pretending. I did not know that.

Less than a year later and I would be off to college and the opportunity to start a new life, full of new adventures and new beliefs . . . free of pretending.

I could not, however, have predicted that in my stand against pretending, belief would find me.

PART I POSTSCRIPT

A FEW LESSONS FROM CHILDREN AND THEIR STORIES

Since Jesus said "unless you have the faith of a child," it seems fitting to pause a moment to learn from these lovely small humans all around us and to remember the child we once were (and maybe still are).

Before we move on to the next chapter in my odd and wandering journey with God, I want to leave you with a few thoughts about childhood and specifically, childhood faith.

FAITH SHOULD BE IMAGINATIVE.

Jesus once said, "Love the Lord your God with all your heart, mind, soul, and strength."[1] It might have been helpful to us creatively constipated adults if Jesus had also included "imagination" in the list of ways to love God.

Children embrace the thought of God as a lion. That image is helpful and daring and inspiring. I wonder if C. S. Lewis had not also written some of the most transformative theology of his generation, if we adults would even allow the lion stories into our theological narrative.

One of the reasons that our Jesus message has lost its attractiveness in the marketplace of culture is because it has become reduced, cold, and creativity starved. We have become so scared of saying something incorrectly about God that we have limited our speech to only the most well-worn dialogues and tired metaphors. The message is boring because it has, quite frankly, all been said before, in just the same way, with exactly the same word pictures and transitions. The tone and quality of our speech comes off as rote and rehearsed instead of affectionate and inspired. Where is the joy of creative risk in our Jesus speech? If I describe God as a river, a constellation, or a rainbow, will I be accused of being New Age or Universalist or worse?

Metaphor and linguistic risk has historically been the stuff of spiritual transformation. Heck, Jesus pictures God as an unjust Judge, a wind, and a fig-tree murderer. Maybe others would be more interested in our beliefs if they witnessed the courage and creativity that comes with imaginative risk.

STORIES ARE A GIFT.

Like it or not, people are transformed by stories. Stories are the language of the heart. They capture us. Jesus spent much of his life working with fiction. Sure he had a knack for nonfiction as well, but fiction was one of the foundational blocks of his spiritual life and ministry.

In one translation of Matthew 13:34–35 it says, "All Jesus did that day was tell stories—a long storytelling afternoon. His storytelling fulfilled the prophecy: I will open my mouth and tell stories; I will bring out into the open things hidden since the world's first day."[2]

It is no wonder that both the Old Testament and the New

Testament are organized to start with long and lingering stories. The theological documents in the form of letters and prophecy are left for later. The lead foot of both is story.

A CHILD'S FAITH CAN BE TRULY LOVELY.

Jesus called all of us "children of God." He exhorted all of us to come to God with the "faith of a child." And most poignantly he said to adults, "It would be better for them to be thrown into the sea with a millstone tied around their neck than to cause one of these little ones to stumble"[3]

That moment in my grandma's family room was and is real to me. However, as a boy I never talked about it. I only spoke of it a couple times, including the one fateful conversation with my Sunday school teacher. I honestly don't know why I didn't talk about it. Maybe it was because I knew it was a weird story, but if I am honest, I don't think that was it. Honestly, I think I believed that no one *wanted* to hear about it. My faith thoughts were simply not interesting to anyone. People were interested in whether I could name the three men in the fiery furnace and how quickly I could list the books of the New Testament, but I doubted that anyone wanted to know my wondering and stumbling thoughts of faith. (As I write these words, all I want to do right now is go straight home and invite my three young sons to tell me about their stories of faith.)

Additionally, I don't think that children are all that much different from full-sized humans. I think all of us would love to tell of our wandering spiritual musings and experiences, but who really cares enough to listen?

The courage to believe is linked to the ability to share our belief-stories with freedom. The ability to share our belief-stories is linked to the invitations we receive to courageously testify. The invitations don't come unless someone loves us enough to ask and then patiently listen.

MAKE SPACE FOR CHILDREN TO TALK FREELY.

I considered naming this section "Just shut up and listen," but then I thought better of it.

Generally speaking, most of us are horrible at making space for other people to talk . . . not just kids either. I am talking about everybody. We are impatient and frenetic in our communication. I spend most of my time half-listening because I am preparing in my head what I am going to say next, waiting for the slightest pause so I can steal the conversation away.

Kids are different, as I am learning increasingly all the time. Their thoughts are not prepackaged and clean. It takes a while for them to meander through their thinking, the words all bathed in clownish characters and story.

I am ashamed to admit that I like the prepackaged answers. They are convenient. The problem is, there is a good chance that they are not true to the child's heart. I am discovering that when a kid's answer sounds prepackaged, this is the exact moment for me to get comfortable and invite them to just talk. The truth, *their* truth, will take a little time.

To this end, it is helpful to ask them open questions that are not leading and don't encourage prepackaged, one-word answers like "fine" or "Jesus."

What do you think about God?

What do you talk to God about?

Who do you think Jesus is?

What do you think about the Bible?

What don't you like about the Bible?

What kind of person do you think God wants us to be?

LET CHILDREN BE CHILDREN.

Children are trying to put their world together. Stories and imagination are two primary building blocks of that process. It is tempting as adults to want to correct children when their answers are too fanciful. For example, if a child tells you that God speaks to their stuffed bear, this may be the moment to ask, "What does God like to talk about?" as opposed to explaining that a stuffed bear does not have real ears.

Our children will learn to submit and even parrot our beliefs soon enough; allow them the gift of their imagination as long as possible. Even be playful with them when they make strange connections (Pinocchio and Jonah) or tell odd stories. Also, keep in mind that the more we adults talk in stories, as opposed to ideas, the more children will feel free to tell us their stories as well. We may even discover that stories unlock adult faith as well.

GOD LETS CHILDREN BE CHILDREN.

It is very important for me to remember that God invented developmental theory. Education scholars did not invent developmental theory; they are just discovering something that God created. As humans grow, we treat them differently depending upon their stage of development. For instance, when our boys were infants, it would be a terrifying thought to lay them in the middle of the living room and to take off and run errands. However, today, when my seven-year-old disappears for a couple of hours to play with friends, we look at it as a gift.

I would never ask that same seven-year-old to write me an essay on courage, even though he is a very courageous child. Courage is an abstract concept, and though he can write, the concept of a coherent paragraph is beyond his ability. However, I would happily ask him to draw a superhero. As he carefully sketched and colored, I could ask him about what makes a superhero "super."

Ultimately, God is the most important player in each of our spiritual stories. God is leading and guiding each of us, and that guiding includes our particular stages of development.

This also means that God might very well treat us differently and appear differently depending upon our stage of spiritual development.

It is tempting to look back longingly to an earlier time with God and miss the stage that the Divine has us in now.

Let's embrace the stages.

EMBRACE GROWING UP

Last night I was talking to Brandon from Montana. Totally unsolicited, he started lamenting to me about the possibility that God might be intentionally becoming less and less present in his life. "I don't like it," he said. "Why would God distance himself from me?"

I looked at Brandon from Montana and said, "I think God's hiddenness is one of the most frustrating things about faith, but let me ask you a question. Was your dad more tangibly present when you were five or now?"

"What?"

I repeated the question, "Your dad, your earthly father—was he more present and tangible in your life when you were five, or is he more regularly present now?"

He thought for a second, then said, "He was much more present when I was five."

"Okay, how about when you were fifteen or now?"

"Fifteen."

"Now answer this, and think about it carefully. Do you know and understand your dad better now, or did you know and understand him better when you were fifteen?"

Brandon looked straight through me. After a long pause, "I know my dad better now . . . better now than back then."

"Even though he is less tangibly a part of your life?"

"Yes, even though he is less tangibly present."

Into the Dojo by Jonathan Case

PART 2
INTO THE DOJO

EVERYBODY LOVES SUPERHEROES: LITTLE boys love superheroes. Greek mythology loves superheroes. Hollywood loves superheroes.

One of the reasons we love superhero stories is because they are true. Certainly a comical exaggeration of the truth, but truth all the same.

For instance, there often comes a point early in a superhero's life where they receive unprecedented attention and training. This often takes place in a mountaintop dojo or a Fortress of Solitude or some other mythical location. This time is typically unpredictable and catches the character by surprise. This dojo experience is only for a season, a relatively short season, but the time away is transformative and marks the protagonist for the rest of her or his life.

In the dojo, the Master is near. The Master may not be hands-on, but there is no doubt that he is near, like a silhouette in the balcony overseeing the exercises below. The Master is attentive, even directive, though not necessarily tangibly present.

I am not a superhero, I am not even an exceptional normal human. In my case, the closest I ever came to a "dojo" experience was in a location as unremarkable as I am. It was more Smallville than Fortress of Solitude. Mine took place in a small cow-town in the middle of Oregon farm country . . .

SIX

A WOLVERINE, A DONKEY, AND A MIME

I FLED Him, down the nights and down the days;
I fled Him, down the arches of the years . . .
—"THE HOUND OF HEAVEN," FRANCIS THOMPSON

ON DECEMBER 31, 1988, I found myself standing on a corner in a non-descript neighborhood in Portland, Oregon. At the time I had no idea that Portland would become my home more than a decade later. This particular neighborhood was so nondescript that it could have been a movie set for a quintessential American film, and it felt just as surreal as a movie studio facade.

Standing next to me was Lauren. She was a lovely girl with long sandy blond hair. Lauren was from the University of Idaho.

Okay, so what the heck was I doing there, standing on a cold street corner in Portland, in the middle of winter, with an Idaho Vandal? Well (and you are not going to believe this), we were about to perform door-to-door evangelism. That's right, four months into my university experience, having fully rejected my faith, there I was, standing on the sidewalk preparing to do my best impression of a religious zealot.

How the heck did I get there, you ask? Excellent question.

Francis Thompson, the nineteenth-century English poet, wrote a poem called "The Hound of Heaven." The poem was the story of his life. Thompson had done about all he could to run away from God, and according to the verses, God chased after him like a hound. Here is a small excerpt:

> I FLED Him, down the nights and down the days;
>> I fled Him, down the arches of the years;
> I fled Him, down the labyrinthine ways
>> Of my own mind; and in the mist of tears
> I hid from Him, and under running laughter.
>> Up vistaed hopes I sped;
>> And shot, precipitated,
> Adown Titanic glooms of chasmèd fears,
>> From those strong Feet that followed, followed after.
>> But with unhurrying chase,
>> And unperturbèd pace,
> Deliberate speed, majestic instancy,
>> They beat—and a Voice beat
>> More instant than the Feet—
> 'All things betray thee, who betrayest Me.'

I, like Francis Thompson, desired to run away from God. God refused to validate that desire.

When I arrived at Oregon State University, I was looking for a new life. Suddenly I was a normal-sized fellow, no longer the diminutive pip-squeak I had been all my life. I had left family and been emancipated from church and its failed promises. I had no desire to weave any more religion into my story. My pretending was officially behind me. No more make believe. No more games. No more dissonance. I wanted to be free.

It was here, amid the illusion of escape, that God sent his henchmen after me. It happened in the "least churched" state of Oregon, where there are very few Christians running around and far fewer with obnoxious passion for their faith.

As it turned out, I was a magnet to every Jesus freak in the area. It was beyond explanation. I must have had a neon sign on my soul that said, RUNNING FROM GOD. TRY TO STOP ME.

And try they did.

The first day of class, I climbed to the second floor of the hundred-plus-year-old Benton Hall. I plopped down with my back against the windowsill in the second tenor section of the university choir. (Okay, okay, so I was a choir guy. Let it go.) The man next to me was an unassuming-looking electrical-engineering student. What could be threatening about an engineering student? Well, as it turned out, everything.

He swung toward me with a tooth-filled grin and said, "I'm Patrick." His hand was extended toward me. (My friend Caroline says that every person looks like some animal. She fancied herself a penguin. I was a bat, not exactly the most attractive animal on the planet. Our friend Kevin was a weasel. As for Patrick, Caroline said that he was a donkey. Which means that the Bible character Balaam and I were about to have something in common.)

I shook Patrick's hand and said, "Hi, I'm Tony."

"Nice to meet you, Tony. Hey, is there any chance that you happen to be a Christian?" I wish I could say that this is an exaggeration, but it is not. He asked me, just like that, out of the blue.

I wasn't sure how to answer him. "Well, I . . . I have spent most of my life going to church."

"Well isn't this just like the Lord. Here we are, first week of school, both needing new friends, and God sits the two of us side by side in the second tenor section."

Soon Patrick got his mitts on my phone number and it was, "Hey, there is a Christian meeting tonight. Wanna come?" or "I just met two wonderful Christian gals. Let's go get some ice cream." It was a nightmare.

Trust me, I was dismissive of his invitations. I was even downright rude at times, but he didn't care. Patrick saw the world through Jesus-colored glasses. I'd blow him off, and he just kept inviting me along. I couldn't escape. Trust me, the second tenor section can be a very small prison.

Also that first week, I met Greg Vavra, a.k.a. "The Vavs." Caroline would have called Vavs a wolverine and rightly so. He was tall and powerful, with gun-barrel arms and a double helping of body hair. This guy had five o'clock shadow at ten in the morning. The dude was otherworldly.

Vavs was a Jesus-guy, but he was not the sort of Jesus-guy to get his inspiration from Martin Luther King Jr. No, he was more of a medieval Crusades guy: his philosophy was "invade and conquer."

Most weeks, Vavs would come to my room to "invite" me to religious meetings. He was bigger than me and probably five times stronger than me, so it was very, *very* important to me not to upset him. I would do my best to make reasonable excuses as to why it was not a good night for me to join him, but he dismissed me every time. Some weeks he would lay siege in my doorway, "starving me out" until I relented and went with him. Other weeks he was not as patient and would simply wrap his meaty fist around my upper arm and drag me down the stairs, out to the parking lot, and toss me into his "Oldsmo-buick."

More often than not, I would sleep through the meeting, but The Vavs didn't care. I think he felt his responsibility was to simply get me into the room and keep me there, a "you can lead a horse to water" sort of thing.

How do you explain this stuff? These two animals are just a couple highlights from those first months. Why was I repeatedly the primary person of interest to every Jesus-loving donkey-man and wolverine that walked around campus? Was that God? Was that God disguised in these obnoxious characters? Francis Thompson said that God was a hound. Is a wolverine that much of a stretch? I ask you.

When that first semester neared its end, and despite the repeated assaults of God's minions, I was no closer to wanting to darken a church's door or associate myself with Christianity. Yet, the assaults continued.

One day, Vavs came to my room. I immediately tensed up for fear that I was about to be drug to the Oldsmo-buick once again, but instead he dropped onto the loveseat in my small college room and stared at me, his hands folded in his lap.

After a moment of anxious silence, he said, "Hey man, there is a conference that I want you to go to. It will be good for you. It happens over the winter break. You should come."

Will this guy ever give me a break? "Yeah, okay, *umm* . . . I am not really interested . . ."

"What do you mean you're not interested? You don't even know anything about it."

He was right—I should at least hear him out, *and then* I can politely turn him down.

Vavs continued, "It will cost you a couple hundred dollars, but you get to stay at a fancy hotel in Portland. You will get to meet a bunch of people, and we will do a bunch of Jesus stuff together. It'll be great. You need to come."

And then he laid siege once again; this time for more than a week. True to his wolverine nature, he would not give up. I would tell him I was broke, and he would come back the next day having pilfered the two hundred dollars from God knows where. I would insist that my mom held Christmas break as a sacred family tradition and in response, he would dial her number, hold the receiver against my face, and mouth the words, "Ask her, ask her, ask her, ask her."

Power and tenacity are a deadly combination.

So, that is how I ended up on the street corner, somewhere in the city of Portland, next to Lauren. I didn't believe. I was a happy apostate, yet there I was. I was there partly out of my incurable sense of obedience, but also because of a very effective religious Ponzi scheme. The scheme went like this.

Earlier that day, back at the fancy hotel, we were divided into groups and ushered into ballrooms. *Easy enough. I'll play along.* We were then told that we would be divided into boy-girl partnerships. *Done and done; this is my kind of activity.* Then we were asked about our religious experience and whether or not we were comfortable sharing our faith with others: experienced people along the east wall and inexperienced on the west. *West it is.* Across from me on the opposite wall was Lauren. Ding-ding-ding-ding! And that, my friends, is how to catch a fool.

On the van ride to our assigned neighborhood, I learned that Lauren was not only lovely, but she was also a Jesus superstar: fifth-year senior, trained Christian leader, and veteran of numerous missions. These facts did not bode well for our budding romance (I would have to let that go), but it was good to know that I was partnered with a religious ringer.

It was only after we were dropped off and the van had pulled around the corner and out of sight that I learned this:

"By the way," Lauren said, the very look of innocence, "did I mention that I am the 'pray-er'?"

I didn't even know that pray-er (a person who prays) was a word. I quickly deposited this new term into my mental dictionary and returned to the conversation. At first I felt a sense of calm. I may not believe this stuff, but I was pretty sure that a little prayer couldn't hurt.

Lauren could sense that I didn't understand the implications of her revelation, so she explained further, using small words. "Tony, I don't know that you understood me. I am the 'pray-er.' Prayer is my spiritual gift. Do you understand?"

I looked at her blankly.

She explained, "When a team goes out witnessing, one person is the pray-er and one is the talker. Once we begin a spiritual encounter with someone, all of my energy is channeled into prayer. I don't say a word." And then she twisted her fingers in front of her lips like a key locking her mouth shut.

I did not know this. It appears some people pray and some people talk. The universe can be a confusing place. Whatever the case, I was confident of one undisputable truth. I was not one of the pray-ers.

For the rest of the afternoon, Lauren and I visited a few dozen houses. Lauren kept her word; she never made a sound. I, on the other hand, knocked on door after door, greeted strangers, introduced my silent friend, and followed the script we had been given. All alone, I tried to carry on spiritual conversations.

The conversations were shockingly anxiety free. All my life I had been scared to death of evangelism, scared I would say the wrong thing, not have the right answer, or worse, lose the debate and thus bump the other person farther down the road to destruction. But on that cold December day it was different; I simply didn't care. I didn't care how the other person responded or how well I argued. I simply asked the scripted questions and patiently listened to each person's answers. Did this freedom come from the fact I didn't consider myself a Christian anymore? That was probably part of it. But now, feeling back twenty-five years, I believe that it was something more. I no longer felt the responsibility to perform well, nor was I primarily driven by the conversation's outcome. I had given up control, and the anxiety that comes with the need to control followed.

As you can probably guess, nobody I talked to that day had any perceivable spiritual revelations. There were no conversions, just pleasant conversations. A few hours ticked by, and we were back on the street corner again to wait for the van, just Marcel Marceau and me.

PARTICIPATION WITH GOD

Back at the hotel, I went up to my room. I sat on the edge of my bed and looked out over the Willamette River.

There was a feeling in my chest that I could not explain. I had just survived an unimaginable afternoon. I had been manipulated by what felt like cult-like tactics. And yet there was this feeling. It was hard to describe. I felt good. No, wait, it was not good. It wasn't quite peace either. The feeling was "right." I don't mean *right* like the opposite of *wrong*; it was right like . . . balanced. There was an odd sense of balance in my soul. After a lifetime of straining and clawing and forcing God to notice me, suddenly I felt all right.

Staring out the window, I was still not ready to talk *to* God, but I was enjoying talking to myself about God, and that seemed like a step in the right direction.

I thought, *Now if God were around, I am sure that he would be hanging out in Africa with suffering folks, swabbing sores with Mother Teresa, or doing a whole bunch of other things that are impossibly beyond me. But do you know what else God would probably be doing? He would probably be having tons of conversations with people about faith, even normal people from the most normal sort of neighborhoods.* That's when it occurred to me: *Faith conversations; maybe that is a way I can participate.*

It was only then that I was able to identify the "right" feeling. I felt right because I had participated with God. That was it. I had spent the afternoon doing the sort of thing that God might do. Sure, the door-to-door thing was a bit forced, but the conversations were not.

Again, I was not yet ready to commit to God, but that day, I did commit to myself to participate in whatever simple ways I could.

So that is how I entered the "dojo." It took a handful of heavenly henchmen, some compassionate coercion, and a heavy dose of well-designed religious manipulation, but I had arrived at the place of learning. Like it or not, returning to my Oregon cow-town would provide me the training grounds.

My friend Mark Skandrette is something of a spiritual guru in his own right. He says that the definition of dojo is "a place to learn *the way.*" Ironically, Jesus claimed that he himself was "the Way." Could it be that the dojo is both a person *and* a particular place and time?

When I spend time with people, they often lament a time in their life where God seemed close. It tends to be an isolated season, a time long ago, a time now lost. My friend Kathryn is like me; she also spiritually longs for her college years. Unlike me, she went to a prestigious private liberal arts college, but her sensation is similar. If you were to ask Kathryn about her life with God, she would quickly tell you about college. Her eyes dance with the joy of those memories, but that dancing is soon replaced by a look of loss and a tone of disappointment, maybe even abandonment, since those memories seem distant and the sensations lost now.

For some people the dojo is a season of youthful enthusiasm, for others it is a time of courageous submission, and for others it comes through addiction recovery. Whatever the circumstance, the sensation remains the same: God is uniquely engaged.

The idea of "participation" was very helpful to me. It was a metaphor of God-engagement that made sense. God was not tangible or interactive, at least not in the way that I interact with other humans, but it did make some sense. I guess you might say that God seemed "nearby," and that was at least more sustainable than the "secret serum" metaphor or "God game" metaphor.

Granted, my concept of participation was very rudimentary. I was simply having "faith conversations," but at the time, that was paradigm altering. I returned to the cow-town campus still having little desire to attend religious events or to call myself a God-follower. I did, however, carry one simple conviction. I started spending some of my free hours wandering around campus to find people with whom to talk about God. Often they were strangers. I would sit with them and say something like this, "I am trying to figure out what I believe. I was wondering if you could spare a couple minutes to talk." More often than not, my new friend would agree, perhaps fascinated by my unapologetic curiosity. And over the next months, I had dozens and dozens of conversations about faith. Yes, I was trying to discover what I believed through the eyes and insights of these momentary friendships, but mostly I was

resting in God's participating presence. I was practicing faith and practicing it without pretending. That was a nice feeling.

In the decades since, the idea of participation has been a formative model. Sometimes it took the form of being on mission with God.
Later it meant connecting to well-proven forms of historical sign
and symbol. Eventually it dwelled in relationship with unexpected
people: the poor in spirit, those from diverse backgrounds, and the
ever-present "neighbor" that Jesus seemed so dedicated to.

"As the Father has sent Me, I also send you."

—JOHN 20:21 NASB

But a Samaritan . . . when he saw him, he felt compassion.

—JESUS, LUKE 10:33 NASB

*"To the extent that you did it to one of . . .
the least of them, you did it to Me."*

—JESUS, MATTHEW 25:40 NASB

SEVEN

ONE DEGREE OF SEPARATION

Truly, You are a God who hides Himself!
—ISAIAH 45:15[1]

THE THING THAT MADE the dojo unique was not my sense of assurance or any spiritual quality that emanated from me. In fact, I don't think God trusted me much at all. God treated me as a simpleton and therefore left me a very uncluttered world. I think we all need seasons like that, simple seasons. This one had a sense of clarity. Once again, the clarity did not come from wisdom inherent in me, for sure not. Nor did it come from my ability to discern God's voice. In this season, God's communication style was blunt and lacked nuance or need for interpretation. It was the rhetorical equivalent of a baseball bat.

God was not, however, personally present. God's preference seemed to be to keep a comfortable distance (hidden): one degree of separation. During this season, which spanned about three years, I never saw a burning bush or heard a voice from heaven. Never once did I have a dream or a vision containing God's instructions. God's tools of communication were the sort of things that we encounter every day: other people, organizations, or circumstances. Normal or not, God used these things to remove the ambiguity.

God didn't want me choosing from a menu of options. God didn't trust me with complicated theological systems. God's instructions were no more complicated than the message on a bumper sticker or a child's Valentine's card: straight, memorable, nuance free, and to the point.

Looking back, I believe that this dynamic was a great kindness by God. My contemporaries seem to want an actualizing power of choice. There is an addiction in my generation to options. "Don't tie me down." "Don't tell me what to do." However, at least for seasons, I think we need mindless clarity. It is the stuff of early transformation and adaptation. This is why musicians are made to practice their scales for hours on end. They may want to jump to improvisation, but a good master/teacher will make sure they do the unnuanced work. The same can be said for a ballerina practicing at the bar, the mathematician memorizing tables, or the athlete in training camp. All of them want to improvise and create, but first they must learn the way.

So in the dojo, God was near but remained just beyond reach. That doesn't mean that God was not involved. God had ways of letting his desires be known. Instead of speaking to me personally, God communicated through intermediaries.

———

God's intermediary communication began one spring afternoon. It was the end of my freshmen year, and I was finally willing to identify myself as a Jesus-follower. My six months of wandering in self-reflection and engaging in random faith conversations with strangers had actually resulted in personal epiphany, even identity alteration. My honest response to who I was and what I had become was this: I wanted to follow Jesus. I wanted to follow Jesus' way. It was not necessarily a direct submission to the church as a group of people. But it was a peaceful acceptance that the church was a part of my story again. It was my family, and I wanted to interact with it as best I could.

That year, I met an intriguing fellow named Kevin. He was a bit obnoxious and overly opinionated, but he grew on me, and in time, we became friends. One afternoon while I was strolling across campus, Kevin came running down the path behind me, shouting my name. I turned and greeted him with a smile. It was a lovely day and I was in good spirits . . . good spirits that were about to come to an abrupt end.

"Hey man, I have been looking for you," Kevin said with a hand on my shoulder and the other on his hip, trying to catch his breath.

"What's up?" I asked.

"Well, I have been praying about next year, and I have a great idea. I think you should be my roommate. More than that, I think we should get a room in Poling Hall and together be, you know, a light for God."

A couple of things you need to know. First, I hate the word *should*. It just naturally stands my hair on end. Two, I liked Kevin well enough, but the idea of living with him and his opinions was a bit much for me to swallow on a spring afternoon. Three, I had a great living gig already set up for next year, off campus in a place free of the burden of being a "light for God." And four, Poling Hall was a cesspool. It was widely regarded as the absolute lowest rung of campus housing, full of partiers, Cretans, and social misfits.

I thanked Kevin for thinking of me, but told him that I wasn't interested.

As I walked off, Kevin yelled after me, "Dude, I think we should do this. Will you at least pray about it?"

I waved over my shoulder at him. I had no intention of praying.

Later that same day, I ran into Erin. Here is what you need to know about Erin. She was in her mid- to late twenties and worked on campus as a chaplain. She was the most regal of women, the sort of person that impresses before they even speak. You probably know the type. The first time I ever saw Erin was at a religious meeting, and when she saw me she beelined across the room, eyes fixed on me, shook my hand, and told me, "I want you to know that this is a better place because you are here." (I am not making this up.)

Anyway, I ran into Erin. We chatted a bit. It was the most normal sort of encounter. Then Erin chose to ruin it. She said, "Hey Tony, you know . . . it's funny. I was praying for you this morning. I hadn't intended to pray for you, but you just came to my mind. And here is the thought that I had." She stared at me for a minute. I think she was pondering whether she really wanted to finish her thought. "I was praying, and I had this thought. I think it might have been from God . . . so, I think you should move into the dorms next year and live connected to your fellow students. I also think you should consider one of the more forgotten dorms on campus."

I was not happy. I didn't say a word; I just stood looking at her with my head bowed slightly.

Erin continued, "Anyway, that is what I thought God said to me this morning about you. Have a great day."

And she blithely turned and walked away.

By the end of the week, two more people randomly bumped into me on campus, and both of them had the same story. They were praying and I came unexpectedly into their mind and they felt the strong impression that I was supposed to be a light for God in the dorms next year.

It was all the stuff of blind imagination and hysteria . . .

My address that next year: Poling Hall, Room 213.

Some would say it was mere coincidence. What say you?

———

Another day, about a year later, I got a phone call from a couple of respected spiritual leaders. They asked to meet me for coffee, and I was happy to comply. Over coffee they took the opportunity to tell me that they had an assignment for me.

There was a long-standing prayer meeting on campus. It had become the very definition of "insignificant and anonymous." So anonymous that even the Jesus freaks hardly knew it existed. It was the sort of spiritual meeting on campus that even though it took place in a centralized, well-known campus landmark and was advertised through Christian meetings . . . even so, no one attended. I certainly was not attending.

The respected leaders told me that they had been praying and were convinced that I was God's choice to lead the meeting. You need to understand that I was *not* a Christian leader. The totality of my leadership was performing skits at the local Christian gathering. That is it: skit guy. I was not the sort that you put in charge of a prayer meeting. I honestly didn't even like prayer.

I flatly refused, but they insisted that it was God's will and told me to pray about it until God convinced me as well.

The rest is history.

I eventually relented to their assignment. My first step was to call Patrick, who I previously regrettably referred to as Donkey Man, a sad misrepresentation of one of the most spiritually significant souls I have ever known. Patrick and I took arms with one another and committed to show up every Monday evening and pray. We realized it might just be the two of us, but Patrick was resolved to not leave me alone.

Again, it was the most insignificant of meetings. It took place at nine o'clock on Monday evenings. Is there a less significant hour in the week than nine on a Monday evening? The meeting met in the most innocuous of rooms, a disregarded corner space on the little-used second floor of the student center. It would seat no more than twenty. And yet we met. We would talk a bit about God, and then we would pray. And really that is all we would do. It was not the sort of prayer meeting where we would talk to one another for forty minutes and then pray for five. It was a greet-for-five-minutes-then-talk-to-God-together-for-forty sort of meeting.

There was very little pomp and no circumstance. We would simply pray—no program, just prayer.

A surprising thing happened: others wanted to participate too. I cannot overemphasize how "boring" the meeting truly was. It started with Patrick and me and a ragtag few. Within weeks it had grown to ten or fifteen, and within a couple of months it had grown to dozens.

The numbers continued to grow. We had to change rooms, then change again. Soon we filled an interlocking three-room space. The time extended from forty-five minutes to more than an hour and began to intrude into the night. Every week without fail, the room was full, bodies piled against one another, every chair taken, and the tile floor stacked with bodies as well. These were college students: stressed-out engineers, jocks, fraternity guys, dorm rats, idealists, and pragmatists all filling the room, praying together. We tried to embrace God and believe that our state university could be different, that God wanted it to be different, and somehow that we could participate with God in that difference-making endeavor.

Campus pastors actually started to cancel other meetings on campus during the week so students would prioritize the boring Monday night prayer gathering.

Our prayers were the language of our faith, and people came.

We had grown to believe that we could actually change the world. This sort of talking to God—and to be honest, talking to God was a lot more about sharing our dreams for the world to God—I would love to say that it was an interactive experience, but it wasn't. Truth be told, outside of an occasional tingling on the back of the neck and a suspicious sense of the Spirit's presence, we were just a chorus singing our desires to the skies.

However, if I am going to be completely honest, there was one spiritual sensation that stood out to me as interactive, maybe even supernatural. It is a secret that I have kept to myself for more than twenty years, but I will share it here for the first time. I have not shared it before because, quite frankly, it never came up. No one ever asked me, "Tony, have you ever had an unexplainable anatomical experience with God?" Such a question was very inconsistent with my religious traditions and cultural pragmatism. Tossing tradition and pragmatism to the side, here is my secret. Sometimes when we would pray together (and it only happened when praying with other people), I would have my eyes closed and my hands clasped in front of me. In the midst of praying, my hands would inflate and become soft. They felt like and took the size of boxing gloves interlaced together. It was an undeniable sensation, and when it happened it would drive me even deeper into focused pleading to God for the people and needs of the world. It felt like God's Spirit was blessing my prayers. Whenever I opened my eyes, my hands were their normal size, not large and soft as I had felt during prayer. It was as if I had been feeling a spiritual version of my hands, not the physical ones.

This sensation happened only from time to time (and stopped once I left the dojo). I am not a charismatic person, at least not in the religious sense of the word. So, what do I do with this? Have you ever experienced anything like it . . . a spiritual sensation that felt like an affirmation from the heavens? Do you think it could have been God, or was it just a manifestation of spiritual projection?

I know that I want to doubt such things. Sometimes I wonder if I have relegated my God-life to paint-by-number when the Spirit wants to dance me through the Louvre.

———

One degree of separation; that is the way that God chose to speak in this season. Why did God stay at this "nearby but not tangible" distance? Was it for God or for me? Was it perhaps a sweet spot that I could handle, sort of like the earth orbiting the sun?

I read once that the earth is on a very specific and precarious path around the sun. If the earth were to move just a few degrees farther from the sun, it would no longer be able to sustain life. Also, it would lose its attractional equilibrium and would go spinning away, out into the darkness with no hope of returning. During my time in the dojo, I certainly had a history of running from God and a tendency toward doubt. Maybe that is why God chose to stay fairly close. By nature, I am a runner, and if given enough of an excuse, I am liable to bolt, but I never got the chance. I was often catching God's shadow just after turning the corner, beyond my sight. Close enough that I was reasonably convinced God was there, just never direct contact.

So, I am starting to imagine why God remained *near* (to keep me from spinning away), but why not *tangible*? Why did God maintain one degree of separation?

There are two challenges to the earth-sun relationship. One is that the sun's gravity would loosen and allow the earth to drift, resulting in a lost and disconnected planet. The other challenge is this: the light and the heat of the sun is the very lifeblood of the earth. It is the nourishing and sustaining presence of this planet. With something that nourishing, you would think that the earth would want as much heat and light as it can get. Right? Why wouldn't the earth desire a double helping of the sun's light and heat? That is a reasonable desire. The only problem is, if the earth were pulled even a few degrees closer to the sun, the earth would burn up. It simply cannot handle closer contact.

It is not the sun that requires a reasonable distance; it is for the earth's good that the distance is maintained.

EIGHT
OF NO EARTHLY GOOD?

He walks with me and he talks with me and he tells me I am his own.
And the joy we share as we tarry there, none other has ever known.
—"IN THE GARDEN," C. AUSTIN MILES

BEFORE WE DIVE INTO this chapter, there is an important concept that I want to plainly confess. Two dear characters that appear again and again through these stories are Kevin and Patrick. They have both been decades-long companions of mine along this journey of faith. Here's my confession regarding my friends: they do not remember these stories the same way that I do. For the most part it is just a detail here or a detail there, but other times the discrepancies are profound.

Kevin, when he looks back more than two decades, may not remember these events to be as dramatic or as spiritual as I do. "Are my memories accurate?" is an important question. However, it is actually more transformative to ask, "Why do I remember my memories *the way* that I remember them?" This is the more revealing reality when processing one's story.

My memories are a museum in my mind.

They are curated by my soul. Like a museum, my soul (assisted by my subconscious) has been careful, even delicate, in the organization and restoration of my memory masterpieces.

My soul is ever-trying to hold together certain spiritual beliefs, and out of self-preservation, it needs historical data to support my particular paradigms. When it comes to our spiritual legacy, most of that data exists in us in the form of story. These stories are the theology of our personal spirituality.

In my case, those dojo years are very precious to me. It was a time when God seemed reasonably near, and I need my memories to support that fact. I need to believe that God was leaving me breadcrumbs to follow. My soul has thus built a theological monument around those years. Do I remember them accurately? Of course not. That does not mean that I remember them falsely either. But I must consider the ways that my inner dialogues about God, both back then and now, affect the historical data of my memories. Kevin, on the other hand, has had a very different spiritual journey than I have (which you will learn more about soon). In light of his self-preservation, he has curated his memories in a certain way, along a different path than I have.

If I am psychologically honest with myself, I must admit my capacity to mix myth (a story that emphasizes meaning over details) with history in light of my spiritual needs and soul longings. Again, I am not saying that I necessarily believe lies, but I must admit the capacity to intertwine myth with memory or to remember details from a certain perspective. There is a very real chance that I cannot trust my memories about something as precious to me as my spirituality. I have a desperation for God: for God to be true, for God to be real, for God to be present, for God to be with me, and for God to be guiding me.

As your stories pop into your head from your own spiritual legacy, ask yourself these questions: Why have I held onto these particular memories? What purpose does each memory perform in my personal narrative theology? Why has my mind and soul chosen to curate these memories in the particular form they hold today?

Now off we go, to another room in the museum of my memories.

———

By the end of my sophomore year, I was in full God mode. I was enraptured with God. There is no other way to put it. I loved my Bible so much, it was like ESPN, a girlfriend, and bacon all wrapped into one. I would fly out of bed every morning, often after only a couple of hours of sleep (because of a long night of God-talk), in order to open that beautiful book. The Old Testament, the New Testament, the Psalms. All of it felt alive and profound. I finally understood what the Bible writer meant when he/she said the Word of God is "living and powerful."[1] My euphoria was about more than just isolated spiritual experiences like reading my Bible in private. It was a daylong dance. Every new friend was a spiritual relationship. Every conversation was a chance to talk about Jesus and the story of the cross. Every school assignment was an opportunity to explore God's ways. I honestly didn't even know I was doing it; the intoxication was so strong.

I remember one afternoon Kevin and I were walking back to our dorm room in Poling Hall. He just kept shaking his head and laughing at me, but not explaining why.

"Are you going to tell me, or are you just going to stand there and grin like an idiot?" I said it to him playfully, trying to goad him into talking.

Once he stopped chuckling enough to talk, he said, "Dude, you have lost it. Seriously, you have lost it."

We had just been in a meeting with our boss. Kevin and I worked for a sorority as dishwashers, waiters, and whatever other chores the girls demanded we do. They called us "house boys," which was demeaning enough, but Kevin and I referred to our position as "dirt slaves," a regrettable name now, but that was the term we used at the time. Despite the name, we actually liked the job, at least mostly. Even so, no nineteen-year-old likes to take orders, even if it was from beautiful coeds.

Our boss was the housemother, a woman named Ms. Barbara. She had invited us in to talk about well, something . . . who knows now. She was a serious woman and not prone to fraternizing with the help. Kevin and I liked working for her well enough, and I am sure it was just a routine management check-in.

But walking home that day, Kevin didn't seem to think it was routine at all. "What the heck did you think you were doing in there? You are going to get us fired." Kevin is the sort of person who doesn't really care if he gets fired, so for him it was all just humorous. "Dude, Ms. Barbara invites us into her office. She is giving us critiques of our work, and all you can do is tell her about Jesus. You wouldn't shut up."

"That is not true!"

At that, Kevin laughed harder. "Yes, it is true. Yes it is. You just can't see it. You are seriously losing it."

I couldn't believe it. "I may have mentioned Jesus once, maybe twice, but it was not *that* big a deal."

"No, you tried to convert Ms. Barbara. Convert her! You were sharing the gospel. And"—more laughter—"she had no freaking idea how to respond. It was awesome . . . and incredibly awkward. *Aaaawwwwk-ward.*"

Around this time, I also started missing classes. I had never cut class before, never. Not in high school and not in college. Never! But suddenly I was missing classes almost every day. I was not missing them on purpose. It was not like I would wake up in the morning and say, "Hey, I think I am going to blow off school today and waste my tuition." What would happen is I would get entangled in a conversation about God and I would misplace the afternoon, the way that we might forget where we left our car keys. It would just disappear. The conversations always ended the same way, with me looking at my watch and saying something like, "Zoinkies! How did it get to be so late?"

It was sort of like walking around in a daze. I was coherent and conversational, but still I was missing things, important things.

This may not have been the best time for me to start my first block of student teaching. I was an education major. All I wanted to be was a teacher. I figured I would teach history to junior high kids. Nobody cares about junior high kids. I know that I felt lost and ignored when I was twelve years old. What better place to spend my life than with a forgotten group of kids?

So for a whole semester I spent my mornings shadowing Ms. Ward at Mountain View Junior High School. It was fun. She was spinsterly but kind enough. I liked working with her and I loved the kids in her class, especially the rough-and-tumble kids. There is nothing better than seeing a flunking student take home a C.

There was something about me that was misfiring though. I don't know what it was, but I must have been missing the reality all around me. I couldn't see it, but apparently Ms. Ward could.

Toward the end of the semester, Ms. Ward pulled me aside. The conversation was abrupt. She was visibly agitated. Ms. Ward told me that I was the worst student teacher she had ever worked with and that she would take it upon herself to ensure that I never saw a classroom of my own. I was shocked. If you had asked me, I would have said that we had a tremendous working relationship and that my time at Mountain View Junior High had been nothing but positive. But Ms. Ward saw things differently. Shockingly differently.

Her final words to me were terse, impatient, and quite frankly, angry. I was told to never return to her classroom again under any circumstance. Her salutation included a promise that she would contact my professors and make sure I was removed from the education program.

I remember walking out of the school building toward my car. In my hands was my small collection of belongings from her classroom: some school supplies and a few file folders. *What just happened?* Ms. Ward had made it very clear that I would be "blackballed" from the

Oregon teaching program. By the end of the week, I learned that Ms. Ward's critique of me was so harsh that even if I applied again in two years, there was almost no hope of being readmitted into the program.

What was I to do? I had just spent two years as an education major. It is hard to give up a dream.

Around this same time, I was walking across campus one sunny spring morning. My path had taken me through the large grass courtyard in front of the student center with its grey facade, tall domed roof, and wide stone steps. To the east of the courtyard was a large red-brick throughway, forty feet across and stretching from one campus boulevard to the other. It was canopied by long, green boughs, and the morning sun speckled the bricks in leopard spots of light.

That was when I heard the commotion.

There was a man, a fellow student, pacing and flapping in the speckled light. I knew him, not well, but he was an acquaintance of mine. His name was something like Andy. He had a Pacific Island heritage, as I recall, and I think he had been on the wrestling team at one time. I remember he was a kind person. He had always struck me as a gentle soul, but not that morning.

He was herking back and forth across the courtyard. His voice pulsated from mumbling to shouting. His eyes fixed on the bricks beneath his feet.

A dozen or so people circled around him, and at least a few were close friends. They were giving him a comfortable cushion to move about. They appeared afraid to get too close. His friends had their hands up and palms extended toward him and they were trying to, I guess, talk him down. It felt very much like a man on a ledge, but he had no place to fall.

As I came closer and closer, I began to hear the exchange. Andy was ranting. "Hell, man! We are talking about hell. This is not a joke! This cannot be ignored. God cannot be ignored. God spoke to me! God spoke to me. God spoke to me. And what are we doing?! What are we doing?! Are we just wasting our lives? Are we just dying for nothing! People are going to hell."

"Andy. Andy! Listen to me," one of his friends was trying to get through to him. "Andy, when was the last time you slept?"

"Sleep. Sleep? I don't know . . . a couple days maybe, maybe more . . . I don't know. Wait a minute! Wait a minute! Don't confuse me with these . . . That is a distraction. A distraction! Sleep doesn't matter. Sleep doesn't matter! Only God matters. God wants me to tell them! I must tell them all!"

Then Andy started to wheel in a circle around the courtyard, like a child's airplane on the end of a string, shouting up at the windows of the buildings all around. "God loves you! Don't you know that God loves you! Come down from your classes! They are a waste of your time. Come down here now and I will pray for you and we will go to heaven together."

His words were so passionate, laced with agony. When he screamed about the cross, it was as if he could feel the nails himself. Andy shook as he pleaded. At one point his knees gave way beneath him. From the ground he stared to the heavens with his arms held wide. Some friends tried to approach, but he immediately pushed them away, half stood, staggered a few strides, and pleaded to the buildings again.

Over the next hour or so, the crowd grew and grew. I don't know if Andy could even see all the people, both friends and strangers. He was enraptured in his God-fueled madness.

Eventually the police arrived. They tried to talk to him as well, but it didn't help. In the end they forcibly subdued him. Andy was strong and a fighter; the submission did not come quickly or easily. I can still hear his wailing from under the pile of officers. He pleaded that they would not take him. He begged that they not stop God's work. He screamed out to God to rescue him. His aching voice filled the campus, bouncing back and forth between her brick walls.

I never saw Andy again.

———

There is a scene in the Bible where Moses meets God. It is one of his supernatural face-to-face encounters. In the scene, after his mountaintop God encounter (the very sort of encounter that I lament I never get to experience), Moses comes back down to be with the people, back to the "real world." But he can't engage like a normal person. Moses must cover his face with a veil because the people cannot bear to look at him. Moses is separated from the community because when you encounter God, it can seriously mess you up.

It was not much better for Isaiah when God showed up. He fell to his knees screaming, "Woe is me," and then he got a hot coal placed on his lips. Ouch. At the Mount of Transfiguration, Peter, James, and John turned into a bunch of babbling morons at that heavenly scene.

These are just a few of the greatest hits of God encounters. Is this really what we want? Is this what happens to us when we encounter God? Do we become like Icarus, flying too close to the sun?

———

My dojo years are decades behind me now. There were times in those years when my faith placed my job or my major at risk, and more than a few times it affected my grade on a midterm. I have since learned my lessons (for better or for worse). My faith life is much more "appropriate" now. It is shrewd, measured, even political. I have not since risked my employment because of religious zeal. I have not detached from the trappings of everyday life. And unlike Andy, I have certainly not risked being publicly ostracized or subdued by police. They say that we can be so heavenly minded that we are no earthly good. I have certainly maintained my "earthly good." I can say that.

These heavenly minded sorts exist, though. You can be sure of that. They are all around us. I see them almost every day. Here are a few of those heavenly characters.

There are folks who shout out the way of God and declare their unique connection to God. Of course, most of them are standing on street corners, wearing shoes that don't match or dressed in a robe or a sandwich board sign. These people cannot get jobs. They often struggle to find food or shelter, but they preach because they feel they must.

There are others who scream at me through my television screen, wearing Elvis hairdos and Liberace suits. Is this who I want to be? If I "encounter" God, would this be my fate?

They do not all demand the stage though. In every church there are the few who "hear from God." For some reason they are never promoted to be on the church board, nor are they asked to run the Sunday school program, even though they make it repeatedly clear that they are available to do the Lord's work. These folks often wear outdated clothing. They hand out inspirational messages on cards with Thomas Kinkade paintings, and they may have an affinity for porcelain Precious Moments figurines. They speak in super-Jesus-talk. They always have a "word from the Lord" for you. They often want to pray for you, and their prayers are usually loud and as public as possible.

I am not talking about people who blow up buildings here; these are just everyday sorts of people in everyday settings. By and large they are harmless folks. But here is my question: Do I want to join their ranks? If I start having mountaintop encounters with God and Shechinah moments, will this be my fate? I have a family to care for, and I like being liked by others. I want to be seen as "normal," even cool. I don't want to become a punch line or someone that people try not to make eye contact with. I don't want to be someone that people "grin and endure." I know I don't want that.

Here is one final idea to ponder. I think we can get lost in God, seriously lost. What I mean is this: we can't handle God in all of God's godliness. I wonder if God gives us such a veiled view of himself because that is all we can handle. The few times that God dares to pull back that veil, more than a peek, we humans end up hiding like Moses or stumbling around a mountaintop like Peter, trying to build a teepee.

Maybe it is because of God's love that God keeps distant. As long as we are wearing these meat-suits, as long as we exist "under this sun" and in this groaning in-between state, maybe we just can't handle full disclosure.

God knows better than anyone what might happen if we fly too close to the sun.

NINE
THE OTHER SIDE

So we fix our eyes not on what is seen, but on what is unseen,
since what is seen is temporary, but what is unseen is eternal.
—2 CORINTHIANS 4:18[1]

THERE IS A SECRET version of me that runs around inside of my soul. This version of me is so secret that I am mostly not aware that he is there. This secret-me is the one who works to fulfill my deepest affections, my longings, and my desires that exist layers below the vulgar and plausibly functional desires that run my everyday life.

This deeper-me is a complicated bloke. In an odd way, you could say that he is my protector. Sometimes he fights for the best version of me, overriding my base desires because of a greater sense of self. For instance, in a moment of titillating temptation, the deeper-me sometimes rushes in and screams, "What the *freak* are you doing?" and chases me out the door.

Other times he protects me by sabotaging my moments of hope. Deeper-me tells me to disengage from my high school reunion because of self-protection. Sure, the room is full of dozens of opportunities for relationship and connection, but deeper-me weighs the cost and decides it is safer to run from that sea of faces that had twenty years before made me feel stupid and small.

Just to help you understand a bit more about deeper-me, one of his jobs is to keep a file of excuses. He keeps them close at hand for my innumerable moments of foolishness.

The deeper-me led me to my wife, insuring that I found someone who is strong enough to stand up to me and hardened enough to deal with my voluminous baggage over our oft-challenging years together.

Let's cut to the core of our topic. The deeper-me also steers my relationship with God. He is a protective force. The deeper-me is ever "counting the cost," mostly in the self-protective sense of that term. He helps me hold onto my pet vices. He helps me not derail my life into a state of "no earthly good." He filters whether it is worth being perceived as a fool. He weighs the losses that come with a life without a secure career or discretionary income. And I suspect (and this is my point) that the deeper-me has insight into the "unseen" world that everyday-me chooses to ignore. Deeper-me knows that I desire a more intimate life with God, a more tangible life with God, but is that life worth the cost? Do I really want what comes with a true knowledge of the unseen world?

That is the job of deeper-me. He counts the cost.

———

There we were, sitting in the cavernous innards of some megachurch in Makati, Manila, Philippines. We had only been in the country for a few weeks. Above us, the ceiling rose and rose to the center like a grand circus tent, opaque and strong with minimal ornamentation. That ceiling looked down on a spacious contemporary sanctuary with its broad front stage and wide pews wrapping around it, spaced like ripples on the surface of a pond. The room was created to hold hundreds, and I imagine that our little group went mostly unnoticed by the lofted stillness above.

We were seated in clumps across the front of the sanctuary. Nerves were fully cocked. We mostly spoke in whispers. The word "terrorists" repeatedly broke the din; our voices punctuated that word whenever we spoke it, even in our hushed tones. Some people's words were seasoned with adventurous exhilaration, others with debilitating fear. Regardless, all of us were hanging on a ledge.

Our leadership told us to gather at this church. That was it, just a time and place. After two days of being sequestered in our hotel with little explanation, here we were. I was happy to get out for a while, but I also knew that by the time this morning's meeting was over, something essential would have changed. Afterward, I may never view the world the same again.

THE CALL

Six months earlier, on December 31, 1989, exactly one year after my afternoon of door-to-door evangelism with Lauren the Mime, I first learned about the mission to Manila. The Philippines had always been an anonymous place to me. It had never earned even my smallest concern. Southeast Asia in general was a region of the world that held little interest. As a Spanish student, I dreamed of Latin America. The tales of Eastern Europe and the volatility of the Soviet Union filled the evening news each night. Even the Middle East and North Africa felt fascinating and exotic. But the Philippines? What could possibly be interesting about the Philippines? Why would I want to visit there?

I was a young man, only nineteen years old. The world was literally mine to explore. I could travel and do almost anything I could imagine, and yet . . .

That moment, the very moment I learned of the Manila mission, I knew God wanted me to go. It must have been God. Right? Latin America or Eastern Europe could have easily been my imagination masquerading as God-talk, but not the Philippines. It was the stuff of pure calling. The Master made his will known to me. No audible sounds or sensations, but I was sure of the Master's leading all the same.

This call was one of the purer God-moments of my young life, but even so . . .

This story is not about The Call.

THE DANGER

Looking back, it may not have been the wisest time in US history to plan an elaborate mission to the Philippines. The trip was set to take place smack dab in the middle of heated contract negotiations between the Philippine and US governments over military bases, specifically long-held and strategic US military bases on the Philippine islands. Like so much of the world, the Philippines had a poignant and painful history of imperial oppression. Today, like it or not, the US is the great empire, and that made many Filipinos nervous.

No one was more nervous than the determined Philippine terrorist organization, The New People's Army (NPA). They were violently opposed to US occupation of even the smallest portion of Philippine land, and their rhetoric of terror was building to crescendo.

At first their attacks had been against US military targets, but as the months wore on and the desperation of the NPA grew, they expanded their "communication" to include what the State Department cutely refers to as "soft targets." The NPA believed that any American could be a CIA operative, so business people, Peace Corp workers, and missionaries were no longer safe.

The threats were credible, and the State Department strongly advised Americans not to travel to the island nation. As you can probably guess, these terror reports thinned our numbers considerably. What was supposed to be a significant army of young volunteers was reduced to a faithful (or foolish) few.

About the time we were planning to climb on a plane to cross the

Pacific, on June 13, 1990, Timothy Swanson of Cheyenne, Wyoming, a long-term Peace Corps worker, was kidnapped from his Filipino home by the NPA. We didn't learn of his story until after our feet were firmly on Philippine soil. The abduction of this innocent became a symbol of the violence that awaited all American travelers. In light of the tales of Timothy Swanson and others, none of us could claim we did not know full well what we were getting ourselves into.

In early July, after just a few weeks in country, we received a letter. It was hand-delivered to our courtyard-style apartment complex. It was slipped to a security guard and he was instructed to give it to us immediately. The letter was in a manila envelope upon which were written the names of our group's four leaders.

We were told very few details about the letter except that it was specifically directed at our group, that it was considered a credible threat by the State Department, and as a result, it required that we leave the country as soon as possible.

Twenty-three years after my summer in Manila, I received a copy of that letter. It was given to me just this week, from my friend and former leader, Marty Brown. It consists of several pages. Each page contains only a couple of sentences. The writing is scrawled and angry, the words in sloppy red grease pen.

Here is what that letter said:

(Addressed with first and last names of our four leaders.)

LEAVE OR DIE
We give you time
up to (specific date)
or else . . .
What happened to
Timothy Swanson will
happen to you.
Since last April,
8 Americans were

slain by the NPA
. . . more will follow
We know, you Born Again
are funded by the CIA
to win our favor on US BASES . . .
NO WAY!
We have your names . . .
We see you
We surround you
We conquer you
We continue going from house to house,
from one school to another . . .
till you find yourself on the CROSS
NPA
WARNING!
What happened to Timothy Swanson
will soon happen to some of you.

As you can see, this was not something to be ignored. The State Department took it seriously. The US Embassy in Manila took it seriously. Our leadership took it seriously. All were passionately concerned and demanded we evacuate as soon as possible.

This letter was the reason for our gathering in the church that July morning.

The danger was undeniably real, but this story is not about The Danger.

THE OTHER SIDE

After an anxious eternity, sitting on those wooden pews, our leader Bill stepped slowly onto the stage and stood behind the podium.

Immediately, the din silenced and we fixed our focus on Bill and his words.

This is where the story gets fuzzy for me all these years later. Adrenaline was coursing through me, and I believe that most of us spent much of the next few minutes holding our breath.

Bill's words were serious and stern. Religious meetings are notorious for beginning with a bit of levity, but Bill would have none of that. It was a time for sober exchange, nothing else.

Bill began to recant some of the events of the last few days and remind us of the very real danger we had all agreed to walk into. He then spoke of the letter, "It was delivered to our hotel." He paused often, searching for the necessary details without inciting more fear than was absolutely necessary. "The letter is a credible threat. We have shown it to the US embassy." He paused again, scanning the collection of wide eyes and furrowed brows. Many were holding hands across the pews. "I cannot share with you all the details of the letter. But I will tell you this—"

Any of us who were not already holding our breaths, joined.

"The threat letter begins with these words: 'Leave or die.'"

It was at this moment, *this very moment*, while the word 'die' still hung in the air, that it happened. A chunk of the ornamental molding from the ceiling high above dislodged. From the shadowed heights, fifteen meters above us, it fell. It was maybe six feet in length, and it drove into the floor in front of Bill with a jarring shriek. It was the stuff of horror movies.

The moment was so startling and laced with evil that every lung emptied in wail, scream, or sob. That wave of sound turned the air thick. Some buried their faces away, unwilling to look, but most eyes were fixed upon the gnarled chunk of ceiling at the room's center. Thankfully no one was injured.

I scanned the ceiling. It was solid, inaccessible, empty.

As the air thinned and just a few whimpering voices remained,

Bill spoke again, "This is a necessary reminder. (Pause) We are not alone."

I don't know how you feel about spirits. I don't know what you believe, but that day in Makati, Manila, Philippines, none of us doubted that the unseen world is real. None of us doubted that the veil between the seen and the unseen had just ripped open before us. And suddenly the NPA was the least of our concerns.

Well, you will be happy to know that we all got out of the Philippines safely. Some of my teammates returned to the States, but most of us got a chance to continue on to Bangkok, Thailand, where we had many more formative adventures.

At summer's end, back home in Oregon, there was no one that I wanted to talk to more than my best friend, Kevin. Kevin and I had been on a two-year journey of faith together. He was my faith-partner. We had lived together, prayed together, ministered together. It was the sort of friendship that could only be described as "family." As strange as it sounds now, we shared everything, from sports equipment to car keys. We even shared access to each other's bank accounts. Kevin was my brother (and sitting here writing these words twenty-five years later, Kevin is still my brother).

Back home, I found Kevin as anxious to talk to me about his summer as I was to talk to him about mine. I wanted to dive into my stories, especially the one about the supernatural warning at the Philippine church, but Kevin cut me off and said he needed to talk first.

His insistence was uncharacteristic, so I smartly shut up.

Kevin wasted no time. "I am done with God."

"What? What are you talking about?" Nothing could have been more surprising to me. Of the two of us, I felt like I had always been the doubter, the one with the weak faith. I'm sure Kevin could see the confusion in my eyes.

Kevin did his best to explain. He shared about his long-standing doubts, his conviction he could never live up to religious expectations, and his desire to learn how the "other half" lives.

I listened, trying to understand. I knew his life story and the hurt that underpinned every word. I asked qualifying questions, but I fear I was more of an annoyance than anything else.

"There is something else." At this point, Kevin's whole demeanor changed. Up to then, his thoughts had been reflective, careful, even bordering on ashamed. Now, Kevin stared right into my eyes and said, "Something happened."

"What? What happened?"

Kevin sighed. "One night, early in the summer, it was the middle of the night, I had the scariest experience of my life. I was laying in bed somewhere between sleep and being awake and"—Kevin groped for the words—"Something . . . *something* came at me."

"What the heck?"

"It started in the hallway, just outside my door. There was a sound like a hot wind. I could hear it inside my head. Then it rushed into my room. It was paralyzing. I was sitting up slightly with my back to the door. I couldn't make myself turn around to look at whatever it was. It just came at me. I can only describe it as pure evil. The evil struck me in the back of the head. I tried to move, but I couldn't. It washed over me and through me. All I could do was take it. Inside I begged whatever it was to stop."

Hearing him tell the story, I could see the scene. Inside I was feeling what Kevin had felt. I was afraid for my friend. "What did you do?"

"Eventually the presence stopped its assault. It had lasted maybe a few minutes or even just a few seconds; I honestly have no idea. I thought it would never end. I couldn't stay there anymore. Once I could move again, my fear ripped me from my bed. I ran out of my room. I ran down the stairs and out the door. I sprinted through the streets only half dressed. I didn't stop running until I got to Clark's house. It was the middle of the night, but I didn't care. You know how Clark is always up until the craziest hour." We both chuckled because we knew all about Clark's unusual relationship with time. It was a much-needed break from the soberness of Kevin's words.

Once the humor passed, I asked him what happened next.

"Well, of course Clark was awake. I told him what had happened. He listened. I think we may have prayed for a minute. I honestly can't remember now. And after a long while I managed to fall asleep on his couch."

"And then?"

"Well, I didn't sleep much for the next few days. I was too afraid."

Kevin and I talked for a long time that evening. We talked about his experiences and what he thought the future held. In the end, Kevin bluntly said what he had been setting up all evening, "Tony, the spiritual scares the s*** out of me, and I am not f***ing around with it anymore."

———

There is a deeper-me that runs around inside of my soul. This part of me is so secret that I am mostly not aware that he is there. Deeper-me's job is to protect me.

The summer of 1990 gave deeper-me a lot to process, and nothing was more urgent than these first encounters with evil, an evil that was as tangible as I had ever wanted God to be.

Throughout these events, deeper-me was counting the cost. Do I really want God to be tangible? Do I really want God to be an interactive presence?

My new reality was this: if the door cracked open between the seen world and the unseen, if God and I started talking more readily, more tangibly, maybe other beings would try to get in on the conversation as well. Is that a cost I am willing to pay?

I don't like being afraid. That summer I had experienced several moments of breathtaking spiritual fear. Ninety-nine percent of my life, I live in soothing ignorance of anything beyond what I can see, touch, and explain. Truthfully, it is a predictable and comforting world.

As much as I say that I want to interact with God, engage God, even have my own burning bush experiences, right now I am doubting whether I truly want that engagement to happen. In order to justify my reluctance, I complain that God has all the power yet still stays away. But I wonder if God stays away, not because of his desire, but in response to deeper-me's desires. God might know that deep down I have a sense of what that dynamic might bring, and for *me*, not God, the cost might be too high.

TEN
BLESSED ARE THOSE
WHO MOURN

Look, if someone wrote a play just to glorify
What's stronger than hate, would they not arrange the stage
To look as if the hero came too late, he's almost in defeat
It's looking like the Evil side will win, so on the Edge
Of every seat, from the moment that the whole thing begins
It is . . .
Love that wrote the play.
—"SHOW THE WAY," DAVID WILCOX

THROUGHOUT MY DOJO YEARS, the sensation of participating in world-change (delusional as it may have been) was becoming habitual. We were young, insignificant, and locked away in a nowhere town, but we believed in world change all the same. We just didn't know any better (or maybe we had not yet become jaded by life).

I went to college during the approach of the first Gulf War, when Iraq invaded Kuwait, cutely nicknamed "Desert Storm." It was a nerve-wracking time for us. It may not have been as bad as the larger wars and conflicts in history, but we felt the anxiety all the same. In classrooms and walking across campus, there was a lot of talk about the draft. We didn't know how these things worked, but we were nineteen, twenty, twenty-one years old and the thought scared us, rational or not.

The time approached for Congress to vote on whether or not to send troops to Kuwait. It was a significant decision that would impact millions of lives: American, Iraqi, Kuwaiti, and more. We also knew it would impact us, even if we weren't drafted into service (which, of course, we never were). We would certainly lose friends, and the world would be changed forever.

The day before the vote, Patrick and I were walking across campus, having the sort of conversation that only university-aged idealists have. "Why doesn't Congress ask us our opinion about the war? Why doesn't anyone want to listen to our concerns?"

The more we walked and talked, the more we felt we needed to act in whatever way we could. Public prayer had become a regular part of life, and if Congress didn't care what we had to say, maybe God would.

It was around noon, and we walked into the student center and found the reservations office. We told the person behind the counter that we wanted to host a prayer vigil that night and asked if we would be allowed the use of the central student lounge. In our historic student center, the central lounge was royal. It was a huge space, the size of a basketball court but filled with elegant couches, twenty-foot tall windows, rich floor coverings, chandeliers, a long balcony, and two ornate fireplaces, one at each end.

The reservations attendant was uncomfortable with our request. I don't think "prayer vigil" could be found in her policy manual. We explained that we just wanted to host a space for students to spiritually process the pending war.

She took the request to her superiors and soon returned with reluctant permission.

The evening was only a handful of hours away. We didn't have time to make fliers or do much promotion (this was long before social media or even email). We just made a few calls and let whatever students we saw around campus know of our plan.

The vigil was planned to start at seven in the evening, and Patrick and I arrived early. By six forty-five the students started to come . . . and come . . . and come. We didn't know where they were coming from. Word had spread from one student to another, and by seven the room was full; hundreds filled the couches and covered the floor.

Now here is the deal. These were not just Christians. There were atheists, Buddhists, students of every background and creed. We all prayed together. We prayed late into the evening. We asked God to be with us and with the world.

———

We religious folks work very hard to try and conjure up God's presence. We will do about anything we can to infuse enough God-feeling into an event to get people to show up. We use inspirational music, emotional films, and charismatic speaking to try to make the God-magic happen.

If God is real, maybe the mechanisms of spiritual longing already exist all around us. Now if we could only be attune to it.

———

Just last week my phone rang. It was Wilson. Wilson told me a tragic story of a twenty-one-year-old man who had been killed in a car accident. His name was Layne. Layne came from a broken home and an unchurched family. His mom had no one religious to turn to for aide in her dead son's memorial.

Wilson was apologetic. He didn't know who else to call, so he asked if I would be willing to come to the boy's high school on Saturday and perform a eulogy. What could I say? If there is one thing that Jesus cares about, it is a mourning mother and the care of a hurting community.

I arrived at the school and found a gathering of close to five hundred people. After a few songs performed by friends (all songs that would not darken most churches), a loving obituary, and a slideshow of Layne's short life, I climbed the stairs and took my place behind the podium before the large auditorium.

As the applause from the slideshow lingered, I let my eyes drift around the room. Bikers, tattoo artists, and dozens and dozens of young people filled the seats. I wondered how many of them would ever consider entering a church; yet here we were, together.

This is what I said:

I woke up this morning earlier than normal. My first thoughts were about Layne, his father, Jason, and his mom, Michelle. I am not the sort of person for whom peace and faith comes easily. The emotion I felt as I lay in bed was anger. Anger that our young men and young women keep dying. This anger is what my Bible calls the "groaning."

Throughout all of human history and across all cultures, when people are hurting, when they are sad, when they are overwhelmed by the groaning, we have always looked for something to help us understand. We have looked to one another, and that is what we are doing here today.

We humans have also looked to our ancestors for help and for wisdom. When we hurt, we reach into the past and lean on the words of those who have gone before us. I want to try and do that for just a moment now.

Two thousand years ago, a wise and thoughtful man said that if we want to move toward spiritual wholeness, we will celebrate with those who celebrate and we will mourn with those who mourn. Today we celebrate together and we mourn together.

In all of my travels and in all of my studies, I have encountered one person that has consistently captured my loyalty. His name is Jesus of Nazareth. Jesus said, "Blessed are those who mourn." By *blessed*, I don't believe that Jesus meant *lucky*. If he did, that would be a barbaric thing to say. What Jesus meant by *blessed* is that when we mourn, we have a unique opportunity to be on God's wavelength; we have a chance to be tuned in to God. Today you have that opportunity; you have an opportunity to be tuned in to God.

Jesus finished the statement by saying, "Blessed are those who mourn, for they will be comforted." In one of the letters in the Bible it says, "Blessed be the God and Father of our Lord Jesus Christ, the Father of mercies and God of all comfort, who comforts us in all our afflictions so that we will be able to comfort those who are in any affliction with the comfort with which we ourselves are comforted by God."

You see, you are being invited into a spiritual relay race. God is offering you his comfort, and in turn you are invited to participate with God and take that comfort to others.

I went on to quote Jesus' words about preparing an eternal home and finished with Psalm 23.

The point of these stories is this. I was shocked by the diverse crowd that gathered in the student center to be with God on the eve of the first Gulf War. I was equally shocked by the auditorium full of folks who would never go to church, but who hugged me and thanked me for taking the time to come and welcome them into life with God.

All of us religious folks want God to be near. We want people to come to our meetings and sit in a space where there is a plausible suspicion that God might just care about us, might be welcoming us, and might want to know us. We will do almost anything to make it happen.

Instead of planning church calendars with well-fashioned outreaches, elaborate programs, and improved mechanisms for entertainment, what would happen if we just lived so that we were prayerfully prepared to be with people in the God-longing moments that seem to happen all too regularly in this broken and hurting world?

God has already promised to be with the mourning. Maybe God will be with us if we are with them.

ELEVEN
WALK A MILE

In these days, God taught me as a schoolteacher teaches a pupil.
—SAINT IGNATIUS

BEFORE WE LEAVE THE dojo, there is one more theme of God's communication with me that I need to explore. It is a theme that first marked me in the dojo years and has followed me in varying forms throughout my adult life.

Those few precious years in college were full of adventure and discovery. It was not a perfect time, but it will surely always be a high point in my life's journey.

This last theme goes something like this:

There was a group of people on campus that I hated. Well, if I am honest, there were probably several groups on campus that I hated, but there was only one group for which my hatred was visceral. I could feel it when I saw a gang of brothers walking toward me on campus. They were arrogant. They walked with a strut, all distinctly dressed with perfectly coiffured hair.

I was completely prejudiced. I admit it. It was like acid inside me. The loathing was so strong that I did not even want to pray for them.

When we would sit in our prayer meetings to pray for the campus, I could pray for most every group around us with passionate ease (administration, exchange students, artists, dorm-rats, athletes), but I had to swallow hard just to muscle a prayer about this particular subgroup.

This group was frat guys. I know that I am an idiot to feel so strongly about dudes in fraternities, but I did. I hated their lettered sweatshirts. I hated their pins and secret handshakes. I hated their obnoxious parties. Mostly I hated the stories of how they hazed the weak and how they hurt women with their overly sexualized culture (at least according to my prejudiced perceptions). They made me angry, and I hated them.

It is for this reason that I was so surprised when thoughts of fraternities started to drift into my prayers. I would be praying along a very typical and comforting line of thinking about my friends or family or future when suddenly, like a drive-by, the peace would be shattered by a thought of that despicable group.

My friend Ken Wytsma says that the surest way to know if the thought in your head came from God is to ask yourself, "Is there any way I would have had that thought without God's prompting? Was that thought something that could just as easily have come from me?" If I had known Ken twenty-two years ago, he certainly would have been laughing at these inexplicable moments of my prayer life.

At first it was just an occasional frat-guy-prayer drive-by. Pretty soon, it became an everyday event. I would try to scrub my soul of the inkling, but it did no good. The thoughts just kept coming, with greater frequency, and to my disgust, with greater affection. In time, I was not just praying spiritually generalized prayers like, "God, please bless frat guys. I pray that they would know your love." I started praying intimate prayers, the sort you reserve for your closest friends: "I pray for their futures, that they would find their place in the world, that they would find wholeness. God, I pray that they will find wives who will love them and whom they will love faithfully. God, I pray for their future children, please . . ." It was bizarre.

In time, I came to terms with it. I even started to pat myself on the back. Look at how far I had come. Look at how spiritually mature I was. *See, God, I am loving my "enemies"* (even though they were only "enemies" as a manifestation of my self-important imagination).

If only God had left it at that. I thought I had done well for myself and God should have been proud of me. Why couldn't God be content with my progress?

Then the drive-by prayers took a violent turn. Up to this point the prayers had all been objective and distant. I was praying for the people "way over there." They were not *my* people. I didn't hang out with them. I didn't even want to know them. That is when I had this prayer, "Maybe I need to become one of them."

What the . . . ?!

That was not a happy day. I became downright sour, sulking my way around campus, dragging that prayer behind me, "Maybe I need to become one of them."

I had almost no doubt that the prayer was from God. Where else could it have come from? Even so, it was a ridiculous idea. I didn't mesh with that world at all. I was a morally minded, bohemian-leaning, religious zealot, and they were, well, you've seen the movies. Yuck!

In the dojo, the Master's desires are clear, and there is no space for negotiation. Even with my spirit of protest, I eventually surrendered.

I was an upperclassman, not some pimple-faced freshman. I had a fully formed campus life. I didn't need their structures and rules to find my way. I was a man, not a boy, and yet . . . what else could I do?

I put on a pair of khakis and began my pilgrimage across campus with my ego in my hand. I called a guy I knew in a fraternity and asked about joining. And the rest is history. I soon became an upperclassman pledge.

For the rest of my college career, I wore my lettered sweatshirt across campus and on Mondays wore my fraternity pin. I learned the handshake and took my share of the hazing (though they did go easy on me since I was as old as most of the veteran members).

I grew to love those men, really love them. They became among my closest friends. We took care of each other, making sure we all got out of bed in time for morning classes. We led the younger members in late-night study sessions to make sure everyone passed their classes. We talked about life. We talked about dreams. I got to know their girlfriends and their hopes for the future. Many of my fraternity brothers are still my friends all these decades later, and *that* is the greatest surprise of all.

I was not there because I had wanted to be. I was there because I had been led there. Even while keeping his distance, I always assumed it was God who nudged me into those relationships. God led me through his invading thoughts and my inexplicable prayers.

—————

There was a part of my healing that required that I became what I hated. It was not enough to love from afar. It was not enough to pray with unexpected compassion. It required that I live in their space, that I donned the trappings of their culture, that I walk the rhythms of their world.

The apostle Paul once said, "I become a Jew to the Jews and a Greek to Greeks," and it is implied in the language that the same can be said for any culture or context. I had been taught to believe that Paul did this only for the sake of the "Jews" and "Greeks" he wanted to minister to. It was little more than an effective sales technique. Now, however, I wonder if Paul also made these wholesale lifestyle transitions for his own sake. Maybe those radical changes helped him constantly process his prejudices and break out of his stagnant ruts. Maybe he found God in the other's world.

Ultimately, the goal is to live like Jesus, and there is no one else in human history who went to greater lengths to "walk a mile in another's shoes." Jesus crossed eternity. He didn't just put on khakis; Jesus dressed himself in blood vessels, sinews, intestines, and grey matter.

The Word became flesh and blood, and
moved into the neighborhood.

—JOHN 1:14 MSG

Maybe Paul knew that part of his participation in the Jesus-life was to take the risk to be fully with the other, wherever he was and with whomever he was called.

Frat guys were my first foray into the idea that it is not enough to just "love" people. We may need to actually become like them or walk with them, for our own good as much as theirs. And this might, in fact, be the stage where God shows up. It certainly is a place where we feel a desperate need for help.

There are many other groups that I have been taught to hate throughout my life by my religion and my culture: blacks, Muslims, liberals, and homosexuals to name just a few. The efforts to divide people are certainly not in short supply. My hatred for these people is real, if I only have the courage to admit it. The only real hope I have is that God will manipulate me, through my prayers and my choices, that I might find the place of love: present love, walking-with love, Jesus-in-the-flesh love. To make that happen though, I may have to walk a mile in the other's shoes. And that could be the death of me. Lord have mercy.

That process started by walking across a campus; my next step was to leave the dojo and walk out into the world.

Into the World by Jonathan Case

PART 3
INTO THE WORLD

THROUGH THESE PAGES, I have been referencing back to the concept of superheroes. There are a few reasons for that. One is simply because my nephew, Ransom, is never far from my thoughts and he has such an abiding love of superheroes, as I imagine most four-year-olds do. It feels different with Ransom though, because I am seeing so much heroism in him.

Second is the universality of the superhero motif. From Greek mythology to Hollywood blockbusters, these hero-tales have been among the most popular and most formative of all human storytelling.

We love superhero stories. One of the reasons we love them is because they remind us of our humanity. Superheroes remind us of our potential, they remind us we are on mission, *and* they remind us that we are flawed, deeply flawed.

It is their flaw, their fatal flaw, that makes superheroes so enticing. What would Superman be without green kryptonite? What would the Hulk be without rage? What would Batman be without his ever demons? What would Ironman be without his arrogance?

Achilles has *no* story without his heel. Sampson has no story without his hair. The Little Mermaid has no story without her unrequited love (in the real, non-Disney version, she doesn't get the prince but instead sacrifices herself for him).

Even Jesus' story was tragic because Jesus simply loved too much. He may have been without sin, but he was not without "flaw." That is to say that his love was so great that it led to tragedy and in the end, his death. Maybe it is because every heart ultimately longs for Jesus that we are inexplicably drawn to all stories of flawed and sacrificial heroes.

After the dojo years ended, the Master kicked me out and into the world. The time had come for me to find my own way.

It was also time for me, among other things, to explore my fatal flaws.

TWELVE
MERCENARY

Forget safety.
Live where you fear to live.
Destroy your reputation.
Be notorious.
—RUMI

WHEN I WAS TWENTY-ONE years old, just a few weeks out of college, I climbed on a plane and moved to Albania. It was my first stop on a series of international assignments that would eventually fill my twenties.

At the time, Albania had only recently thrown off a fifty-year-old Communist regime, one of the strictest the world has ever known. She was attempting to write a new story, a story inspired by her ancient past, while finding her place in the new globalized world, full of opportunity and freedom.

The deck seemed stacked against Albania, though. They were historically Muslim but surrounded by the Christian West. They were the poorest country in Europe. The whole of the Balkans, at the time, was a political and militaristic powder keg. And five decades of unprecedented totalitarian isolationism had left them ignored and unknown by most of the world.

In spite of all these realities, I arrived to find an undeterred, hopeful, and generous people, and through my early twenties I counted it an honor to stand with them as "family" and friends.

I arrived in country with a ragtag team of American idealists. It was the most courageous group of people I have ever worked alongside. We lived intimately and on edge, as unruly as a troupe of young gorillas. In some ways we were the worst sort of missionaries, all action with little reflection. The slow-mission models that have become so popular today would have been mocked by us. We were high-octane and unapologetic about it. We had not come to Albania to linger; we had come to get business done. And that is exactly what we did. One influential international missions leader once called us the most successful team of young missionaries he had ever witnessed. Purely from a production paradigm, he may have been right. We were industrious and we had the statistics to prove it, but looking back I don't believe the successes came primarily from our prowess.

You see, back in the early 1990s, Albania was a missionary playground. Revival was breaking out all around us. In some ways we could do no wrong. Every idea, every program, no matter how roughshod in its initial visioning, burst into success. The opportunities seemed limitless. We watched conversions happen every day. We couldn't start Bible studies fast enough to fill the need. It felt like an orangutan in a party dress could have drawn a spiritually interested crowd.

And in the midst of that cacophony, I found an intoxicating comfort.

I did not handle those circumstances well, certainly not as well as the others. I was mesmerized by the activity, and I started to believe the press. *Maybe we are super-missionaries. Maybe I could actually do no wrong. What if I am one of God's chosen few?* (Always a dangerous thought, but especially so when conjured up by a testosterone-infused twenty-one-year-old.)

All this was compounded by my fatal flaw.

Many years later, I was sitting at a bar with a young man named Derek. Derek had had some difficult experiences and was dealing with some doubts about his spiritual journey. He had heard that I had lived through some stuff overseas and was hoping that I could give him perspective. I told him that I didn't know how much perspective I had but I would talk him through my story.

Mostly Derek wanted to listen. I told him about my move overseas, fresh out of college. I told him about my experiences in several cultural and spiritual hotspots around the world through my twenties. "It was like I couldn't help myself," I said to him. It was one of those conversations where you leave your normal script and start to wander in unknown and untamed territory.

"Derek, with each move I tried to take on more and more responsibility. It was important to me to have titles and to have others recognize me. It was incredibly important. I worked longer and longer hours, sometimes going months without a day off: language learning, program development, teaching, leading multiple teams, strategizing. All of that was punctuated by the occasional military crisis, terrorism, or the need to dodge the secret police. I think you get the idea. But it wasn't just the work. I was constantly looking over my shoulder at others and wondering, *am I doing enough?*"

"Am I doing enough?" is the language of insecure faith.

It was at this moment that I spontaneously said something to Derek that I had never said before. Heck, I had never *thought* it before. It was the sort of statement that rung with such soul-truth that after it slipped out, I stopped talking all together. The statement was simply this: "I think I was trying to get God to notice me." I could only stare at Derek after I said it, with eyebrows raised . . . surprise and distress on my face.

I think I was trying to get God to notice me.

Growing up, I was not an impressive kid; quite the opposite, in fact. I had some learning difficulties that made school a struggle, and

I spent much of my developmental years in remedial classrooms. I was also an embarrassingly late bloomer. Most of my years I was among the smallest in my class, and I didn't hit puberty until the end of high school. Five-foot-two and a hundred pounds is a tough way to get through a large, affluent, and adept school system. Let's just say, it was easy for a kid like me to get lost, and the opportunities for validation were meager.

I also come from a clan of pioneers. We are old Oregonians, at least as far as white people go; my people had lived many generations in the "frontier." My parents were good people, full of character and generous.

My dad was raised on a ranch, and he had pioneer/ranch values. He believed in hard work. He believed in independence. He believed that actions speak louder than words.

My pioneer dad truly didn't know how to relate to his awkward, quasi-bohemian son, so he did what a lot of dads do—he chose mostly not to relate. Our conversations were few and his affirmations fewer.

I only have five childhood memories of my father speaking his delight to me. The exception was when he witnessed me singing when I thought no one was listening. I turned and caught him staring (I think to his surprise as much as mine) with a goofy little smile on his face. Having been seen, he curtly said, "I like your singing," and then appeared uncomfortable and quickly turned away.

The other fleeting expressions of delight were all for the same reason: I had taken off, journeyed away, vanished out on my own. Each of these times, I disappeared and returned having accomplished something unexpected without asking for any help. Dad seemed to love those mercenary moments of raw and adventurous independence, so much so he couldn't hide the twinkle in his eye, even while reprimanding me for worrying my mother.

Slowly and undeniably I learned that if I wanted my Dad to notice me, I needed to take off. I needed to run away. I needed to leave him behind. I needed to show him that I didn't have to rely on him.

Dad left me with a mercenary mentality.

So when I signed up to be a missionary in Albania, I lied on my application. I wrote down that I wanted to be a minister, a program developer, and a relief worker. What I should have put down was "mercenary," because deep down inside that was what I truly was.

I was fueled by independence, self-reliance, and a need to win battles.

Here is the great irony. Are you ready? You have probably already sensed it.

On the one hand, I wanted, more than anything in the world, for God to notice me, just as I surprisingly confessed to Derek on that barstool two decades later. However, the only way I knew to get noticed was to run away and prove that I didn't *need* the very Person whose attention I most desired. It created an insidious paradox, one that at the time, I could not see. It was simply my lifelong programming.

As a result, all I knew to do was to shift into overdrive, rev my faith-engine into the red, and see how long it would take to burn out. So overdrive was how I lived. I am not saying I worked harder than the others (all of us gave sweat and blood to the work); it was more a measurement of the state of my soul, not the capacity of my calendar.

I drove that way for the better part of a decade.

Here's the real insanity of it, in regards to our discussion of God's hiddenness: I basically lived like God wasn't there. Again, it was not functional atheism; I believed in God. It was just that my belief left God far, far away. Even the spirited prayer life that I had so often experienced in the dojo was all but gone. In all those years living overseas, I don't have one memory, *not one,* of an intimate prayer experience with God. Isn't that strange? It felt like the Master had loaded up my spiritual backpack with all the supplies, resources, and weapons I might need and then pushed me out of the dojo and into the frontier to work and fight on his behalf, but *not* by his side. I was now an agent of the Master's mission, but not a companion in the Master's life.

Then Albania reinforced that paradigm. It didn't seem to matter if I prayed or not. Ministry productivity seemed to happen all around us regardless. My life actually became less and less in tune to God and more in tune to the work.

To try and explain what it felt like, it was similar to trying to convince a twenty-first-century middle-class westerner to view God as Provider. How can you possibly communicate "Give us this day our daily bread" to folks who have overstocked kitchens, job security, and enough investments and retirement stored up to support a dozen families? Who needs God's provision? It is a very challenging dichotomy. We might pray the Lord's Prayer, but does it have any substantive meaning? That is a somewhat awkward parallel to what I was feeling in Albania, where our ministry cupboards were overflowing. And that feeling reinforced my mercenary orientation.

I wanted to believe that I was relying on God and spoke often as if I did, but deep down I was alone, even intentionally so. I was on a mercenary mission to *prove* to God that I was worthy of his attention and love.

THIRTEEN
BUCCANEER MAPS

Knock, and the door will be opened for you.
—JESUS

IN THE DOJO, I was disappointed that God maintained one degree of separation. Even though I was ever-thankful for God's leading through intermediaries, I always wanted more.

It was different after I moved "into the world." I didn't care as much. Interaction was not the arrangement (at least that is how I interpret those years now). In this season, God's job was to sit on his throne on Mount Zion . . . or Mount Olympus . . . or wherever he sat, and watch to see if I made good on my promise. My job was to deliver.

Even though God remained relationally distant, it did often feel like he was stacking the deck on our behalf. To use a different metaphor, God was like the writer of a buccaneer's treasure map. The map existed whether or not the Writer was present. The job of the buccaneer was to manifest the guile and courage to dare to follow the map wherever it led and hope that the end marked God's predetermined treasure. Across the world, these buccaneer maps led us to places as exotic as the capital cities of the Middle East or as provincial as forgotten villages in Albania's rugged frontier. The destinations were always unexpected.

The maps might even lead to the second floor of a Greek embassy.

It was a bright morning and early. I remember that it was a Friday.

Albanians can be very private people, suspicious of strangers, so it was odd when I was startled by the sound of my friend Geni yelling up to my room from the courtyard of my Albanian family's home. He was standing underneath the tangerine tree in our long, narrow, wall-enclosed courtyard in front of our four-room house. There were nine of us living in those four rooms: the most wonderful Albanian family of five on the main floor, and we four foreigners had taken over the upper two bedrooms. We were under our family's roof and under their care. My bedroom dumped out onto a wrought-iron-railing-lined balcony. It led to a tiled stairwell that cascaded down to where Geni was now standing below.

Normally, if an Albanian was not personally known by my family, they would wait outside the courtyard's worn wooden gate for permission to enter, but not that morning. Geni was a particularly polite young man, and yet he had broken cultural protocol. I thought to myself, *something must be wrong.*

I jumped out of my seat where I had been reading and drinking coffee out of a culturally inappropriate mug the size of a teapot. I ran, half-dressed, out onto the balcony and leaned over to greet Geni below.

I called to him with an Albanian phrase that roughly translates to "What's up?" It is a casual greeting between friends, but both our expressions were far from casual.

"I need to talk to you." Geni was blunt and direct as always.

"Yeah, come on up."

I had known Geni since my first week in Albania. He had sort of adopted me. He was a great friend and I had grown to love his whole family. I had spent several holidays back home with him in Korce, a small southeast city, celebrating with his parents and siblings.

Up in my room, Geni didn't want to sit down. He was also not interested in a cup of tea. He pushed his long blond bangs out from his eyes and spoke plainly and urgently.

"I need your help. I have just spent two days standing in line at the Greek embassy trying to get in."

I knew exactly what he meant. Greece stands across Albania's southern border. It is a primary destination for Albanians looking for resources or a new life. The problem was, Albanians were viewed as little more than dogs, akin to Gypsies, in the eyes of most Greeks. Their embassy sat in the middle of Embassy Row, a walled-off and militantly defended section of Tirana, the capital city. Only foreigners were allowed to walk along its pristine and opulent streets. To "deal" with the unending Albanian requests for visas, the Greek government had jackhammered a narrow gap in the thick wall alongside the embassy to control Albanian traffic. The crude gap was rough and low, requiring the petitioner to cower through. The gap was guarded day and night by soldiers with machine guns. The line outside the wall was blocks long, and it was not unheard of for people to wait for days in the garbage-filled alley to gain entrance.

"I have been waiting in line for two days, and it has hardly moved. I cannot afford to wait. I need to get a visa for my mother and sister now, so they can go to a Thessaloniki hospital. There is nothing more they can do for my mother's cancer in Albania. The Thessaloniki doctors are waiting to help her. All we need is the visas."

If you have lived much life at all, you know the desperate look in the eyes of someone who is on the verge of losing a loved one. Now imagine that desperation from someone who knows that hope lies a few miles away, across an arbitrary line on a map, a line they are forbidden to cross.

Geni continued, "I can't get in, I have tried, but you . . . *you* have a US passport. You can walk right onto Embassy Row." He placed his hand on his chest. "We are asking you to represent our family. Will you help us?"

I didn't know anything about embassies or advocating for a suffering family. The thought scared me and severely challenged my pragmatism. Would this even work? What could someone like me possibly do?

Geni assured me that there was a fax waiting inside the embassy that would explain everything and ensure visas if only someone could get in.

For the next few minutes we shared an anxious conversation. Geni was pleading, and I was trying to figure out whether or not this was a buccaneer map I was willing to pursue. In the end, I did what I must. I agreed to go.

Silently we walked the thirty minutes to the guarded entrance. When we arrived, Geni kissed me on each cheek and told me he would be praying. I turned and showed my passport to the guardhouse, signed my name, and the soldier dismissively waved me in.

I was alone in the wide boulevard—no movement, neither cars nor people. Bored soldiers in towers followed me with the nose of their rifles. It was surreal. Two blocks down, I came to the palatial Greek embassy and turned left down to the "peasant" side entrance. There I found another guardhouse and more soldiers. I signed in and was told to stand along the wall. I could see parts of half a dozen Albanian faces peering through the crude crevasse in the thick outer wall.

After forty-five minutes, I was called by the guard and allowed through the tall iron gate. They pointed me to a door on the back corner of the ornate multistory building. I cautiously observed the large yard around me: lovely trees in the back and a garden down the side surrounded by an ornamental fence. I opened the simple door and found half a dozen people standing in a windowless, sauna-sized space. A second door stood closed on the sauna's other side.

I soon learned that the second door opened only once every thirty minutes, allowing one petitioner through at a time.

What the baklava have I gotten myself into?

As the hours passed, doubt replaced my guile and insecurity my anemic courage.

Eventually, my turn came. I was ushered into a large waiting room filled with long wooden benches and, at the far end, a few teller windows like you might find in a bank from a western movie. I got in line behind a few dozen folks, and after an hour-long wait, finally got my moment at the window.

The attendant was haggard and impatient. "What do you want?" His English was excellent.

I explained as quickly as possible the situation and asked him to look into two visas for Geni's family. He was only half listening, shuffling papers and distracted by the activity all around.

It took several attempts to explain my situation. Annoyed, the man told me to take a seat and he would deal with me as soon as he could.

So here is a funny detail, the sort of funny detail that sometimes happens mid-adventure. I took a seat on one of the long benches in the center of the room. I just sat, staring unknowingly around the foreign room. After twenty minutes or so, a regal woman strolled in. She was tall, at least six feet tall in her heels. She had a lightness and grace to her step. When she saw me sitting there, with my long hair and disheveled clothing, she came over to engage me in conversation.

"What is an American doing here?" (Wherever I go, it seems that everyone has no problem tagging me as an American citizen. I wonder why.)

She introduced herself as Katarina, and in return, I gave her my name and told her about my situation. She was notably sympathetic and expressed her genuine concern. Then she took the conversation on an odd detour.

"Do you know the most beautiful place in the world?" she asked. It was an unexpected question to be sure, especially between new acquaintances.

"No, no I don't." I was just happy to not be alone for a minute in that disconcerting place.

"The most beautiful place in the world is a place called Ore-ee-gun. Do you know it?"

What did she just say? Did she say Oregon? "Did you say Oregon?"

"Yes, yes I did. Do you know this place?"

"I am from Oregon. Oregon is my home."

At this she dropped down on the bench next to me and said, "Back at home, I have a picture book on my table. It is full of photos of that wonderful place. Waterfalls, beaches, mountains (she said it with three syllables: "mouw-oun-tins"), lakes, rivers. It is wonderful. Is it truly as beautiful as the photos in my book?"

"Yes. Even more beautiful in person."

With this she smiled and placed her hand on my arm and said, "I will pray for your friends. I will pray that this woman is healed. It was lovely to meet you, Tony from Ore-ee-gun."

Then she left. My encounter with Katarina, as impossible as it seemed, was like an oasis in the midst of that painfully arduous day. *If only I could stay in the oasis forever.*

Maybe forty minutes later, my name was called and the same attendant asked me to explain my situation again. I told him about my friends, and I told him about the fax that would explain everything.

"Okay, what is the number of the fax?" he asked.

"The number? I don't know the number. It is from a Thessaloniki hospital. It is about my friend."

This is when his vapor-thin patience came to an end. He started to yell at me in that "charming" way that Mediterranean people do. "Do you know how many faxes we get every day?" (He didn't wait for an answer.) "Three thousand. Do you know how many visa applications we get a day? Five thousand. And you want me to find one little insignificant fax for *you*? Get out of here. There is nothing we can do."

Then a soldier stepped forward and forcibly ushered me out of the building and back onto the deserted street.

My adventure had been an indisputable failure. There was no treasure to be had, which is always one of the risks. A few minutes later,

I surfaced outside Embassy Row. Geni had been waiting on the curb, squatting down and watching the cars drive by. Five hours had passed.

When he saw me his face exploded with hope.

It was my "privilege" to shatter that hope. "Geni, I failed. I am so sorry."

We walked back to my house in silence. Geni was not disappointed; he was destroyed. I, on the other hand, went back to my work.

The following Friday, I was awoken by the sound of Geni's voice once again. I pulled on a shirt and went out the door. Geni looked up at me; his eyes were wild like a man who had not slept in days.

"I have a fax!" He tried to whisper in the early hour, but his whisper was louder than a normal voice.

"Get up here," I said, rubbing my eyes with the heel of my hand.

Geni explained that he had returned home and they had managed to get a fax from the hospital in Thessaloniki. It was time for me to return to the embassy again.

Oh no, I thought. *I am not going back there. Last time it was more than five hours of total humiliation: rifles pointed at me, stuck in window-less rooms, ignored, treated like cattle, yelled at, insulted. He can't be serious. Five hours! It was five hours.*

I asked him if the fax would really work, and to his credit, he didn't lie. "It does not have all the information, but we need you to try anyway. Maybe it will work. Will you try?"

To my shame, I tried to weasel my way out of it. I tried several times. There is just not a justifiable excuse when a friend's mom is dying. Eventually, his persistence won out and we were off again, trudging toward Embassy Row.

Truth be told, I was furious at this point, not at Geni—he was doing what any desperate son would do—but at the map. I felt like a charlatan had sold the thing to me and it was only going to bring me heartache and more defeat.

We arrived at the guardhouse, and Geni placed his hands on my shoulders. Then he bowed his head and pleaded with God, "God, I pray you will open up a door for my brother."

I looked up to find Geni's face resolute. "Go."

Fueled by Geni's confidence and with rechanneled fury, I walked to the guardhouse, slapped my passport against the plexiglass, and with my other hand reached through the slot, grabbed the clipboard, and signed in, keeping my eyes trained on the soldier inside.

Fax and passports in hand, I marched down the very center of the boulevard, inside daring the rifled soldiers to get into my business.

Following the map in my heart, I arrived at the embassy and turned a hard left. I walked to the next guardhouse, slapped my passport on that glass again, and signed myself in. Then without waiting for a response, I walked to the tall iron gate and let myself in. The guards barely took notice; I am sure I was not the first arrogant American to stomp onto their grounds.

Then I saw it: the sauna room on the embassy's back corner. My courage wilted. My gait slowed and my shoulders dropped.

When I was about halfway to the sauna's door, I glanced to my right at the lovely garden along the building's side. It had a decorative stone path through it and . . . *wait a minute.*

Halfway down the garden was a small side door into the embassy, and that door stood wide open.

What had Geni prayed before I left him? *"God, I pray you will open up a door for my brother."*

We religious folks use language like this. "God, open up a door and I will walk through it." Jesus even said, "I am the door"?[1] This sort of door theology is not new. I, of course, thought Geni's prayer was metaphoric. It had not occurred to me until just that moment that God might have taken his words literally. Literal or not, God or not, the only question now was, *Am I willing to risk, submit to my friend's prayer, and walk through this open door?* It seems to me that much of the Jesus-Way comes down to a daily decision to surrender to such questions.

Without considering the consequences, I turned and walked through the ornamental gate and down the winding stone path, a space clearly reserved for the ambassador and his family. Everything about it screamed "Stay out!" There were delicate flowers brushing my legs and guard posts atop the walls. I chose not to look at the men with machine guns; my eyes were fixed on the open door.

It only took moments to arrive, and I hurriedly stepped through to find only a stairwell to the second floor. I grabbed the railing and pulled myself up the first few stairs. Two-thirds of the way to the top, a secretarial desk came into view and a large woman sat behind it. She looked up to see a bedraggled young man walking toward her, and her eyes burst into fire and she began to scream in Greek.

From down the hallway, two huge men in suits ran out. They met me just as I reached the stairs' crest. Each man grabbed one of my arms and lifted me up to take me back down the stairs and out the door. My feet fumbled for the stairs beneath me.

Just then, a regal Greek woman walked out of an office and into my view. Before I knew what I was doing, I cried out, "Katarina." She turned and saw me being dragged down the stairs and said, "Tony, what are you doing here?"

At the very sound of her voice, the two goons stopped, set me back on my feet, and took a submissive step away.

"Katarina," I said, trying to speak through my pounding heart and desperate breaths, "I need to talk to someone about visas for my friends."

"Oh no. You can't be here. You simply cannot be here." Then she looked around. At this point every member of the second-floor staff was standing in doorways, watching the drama unfold. "Come in here with me." And she led me to a formal office. The plate on the door said AMBASSADOR.

In my daze, I asked, "Are you the Greek ambassador?"

"No, I am just filling the post until the next one is appointed. Now, tell me about your friends again."

I explained all that I knew, and I handed her the fax along with the two passports. Katarina scrutinized the fax, and after a long pause she said, "There is simply not enough here to justify the visas."

I stared at her, but she didn't look up from her reading.

"Would you please excuse me for a second?" and she abruptly left the room.

Maybe five minutes later, she returned. In her hand were two six-month multiple-entry visas in the names of Geni's mother and sister. This type of visa was unheard of, particularly in the hands of common Albanian citizens. (They were like gold, worth thousands and thousands of dollars on the black market. Apparently, buccaneer maps sometimes do lead to treasure.)

Katarina took my hand in hers. "Tony from Ore-ee-gun, your friends go to Greece with my prayers. Now, I am sorry but you *must* leave. You shouldn't be here."

And that was it.

Back out on the street, I was feverish and frail. I wanted to throw up, but I refused to give the rifled soldiers the entertainment. *What did I just do? I could have been shot. I could have been arrested. I think . . . I think I was almost arrested.*

I had been gone less than thirty minutes when I returned to Geni, squatting on the sidewalk. After such a short amount of time, he looked up at me with sorrow, convinced I had failed, or worse . . . his friend had simply quit.

I handed him the passports and visas and said, "I have a story to tell you."

We walked home arm in arm, as Albanians do, and I told him my story. Then we sang songs for the strangers we passed.

———

In these pages, we are asking the question, where is God?

Was this a God story? What do you think? There are certainly plenty of people who would simply chalk up the embassy events to coincidence. Others might dismiss it as luck. It is certainly a dramatic story, but does that necessarily make it a God story? I am asking myself that question. What say you?

Does the fact that I was a Christian missionary (immature, selfish, and belligerent, but still a missionary) make you more inclined to put this story in the God column? How about the fact that Geni's whole family had prayed to receive Jesus as their personal Savior? Does that enhance the story's credibility as divine intervention?

On the other hand, what if I had not been a missionary? What if I had been a secular Mercy Corps worker and Geni was my Muslim translator? Then what? Would those terms infuse more doubt as to whether or not God had drawn the map?

Here is another question: What if I told you that Geni's mom never made it to the hospital, that she died before she could arrive? Now how do you vote: God or not God? Does God intervene in tragic stories as well as successes? (By the way, I want you to know that Geni's mom did, in fact, make it to Thessaloniki, got treatment, the cancer went into remission, she received a few more precious years of life, and she was an unbelievable blessing to everyone she met right up until her last days.)

It would have been helpful to me if there had been a burning bush along the way in this story, from which God's own voice assured me that following Geni on this adventure was God's divine will for me. Burning bush or not, there sure seemed to be clues left for me at each step along this path. Thank God that, with each new clue, I took the bumbling risk to dare each new step.

FOURTEEN
REPEATER

As for me, the silence and the emptiness is so great that
I look and do not see, listen and do not hear.
—MOTHER TERESA

IT WAS MY SECOND summer in Albania. Actually, it was technically late spring. Leon and I were driving up the side of a mountain in a vehicle that could have easily navigated the Sea of Tranquility if called upon.

We were in the mountains of Albania's rugged north. We weren't just in the mountains; we were on top of Albania's roof. Our mission was straightforward. We needed to find a secure location for a repeater. What is a repeater you ask? Well, thank you for asking. A repeater is a box, the size of a small suitcase. Inside the box is a device whose sole purpose is . . . wait for it . . . to repeat. I know, shocker.

Back in those early days, communication in Albania was very rudimentary. This was before cell phones, but honestly, reliable rotary phones would have been a leap in the right direction. In the capitol city, if I wanted to call my parents, I had to walk to the city center and climb in line at the post office, where I would wait, sometimes for two hours. When my turn at the phone came, I would begin to dial my parents' number over and over, sometimes dozens of times, before I would luck into an open international line. At the time, there were only a few of these lines out of the country, and they were terribly overtaxed. So, if I wanted to fulfill my sonly duties and reassure my mom that I hadn't been captured by terrorists or contracted dysentery, I had to block out a good three hours, just to be safe. Back then, a call cost close to a dollar a minute.

But Leon and I were not in the technologically advanced capitol city. We were in the Albanian outback.

In order to accomplish our village work in the rugged north, we used VHF and HF radios. It was technology that seemed more WWI than Desert Storm, but it was what we had. Unfortunately, because of the vertical terrain and the radios' reliance on line of sight, we had to place the repeater box on the highest crest possible. From that elevated place, the device would capture an incoming radio message from one side of the mountain and retransmit (or "repeat") it down the other side of the mountain. It made for clumsy communication. If I wanted to radio someone using a repeater, I had to speak one phrase at a time into the handset, wait in silence while the box recorded and restated my message, then, as the other person responded, there was silence as the repeater captured their words, and then finally I would receive the response. Let's just say, this type of transmission rewarded an economy of words.

When we arrived at the mountain's rounded treeless top, we found to my surprise a small military installation. There was a two-story building at the middle of the compound and several small surrounding support structures. The base was encircled by a crude but intimidating barbed wire fence. There was only one gate in.

The sound of our moon vehicle had aroused the base's lone inhabitant. He huffed out to the gate as excited as a springer spaniel. He was so delighted to have visitors that he had forgotten to bring his rifle. As he ran toward us, he tucked the tail of his shirt into his pants. His belt buckle, a holdover from an earlier time, still carried a communist star.

The poor chap was unlocking the gate before we even had time to complete our pleasantries. This isloated soldier had already completed the meaty portion of his six-month assignment at the remote location. He had been left there without a vehicle and assured that he would be relieved half a year later. Can you imagine? The poor guy was relationally starving and probably would have invited a hostile takeover if it meant we could share a small meal together first. He frantically waved us to follow him into the two-story building.

He talked at us a million miles an hour. I was able to catch only about 90 percent of it. My Albanian at this point was pretty decent, but his particular dialect and accent proved a bit challenging.

He made us a cup of tea, and we sat together around a tiny table and sipped. We knew we wanted to ask him if we could leave the repeater on top of one of the installation's outer buildings, but that request could wait. Right now, the poor guy just needed us to be his friend, and we were happy to comply.

About halfway into our visit, he leaped out of his seat. Literally. He actually left the floor with excitement. He waved to us to follow him and scurried out of the room. We went through a few small passageways and came into what must have been the heart of the small base. Inside were a handful of communications devices.

Our new friend walked to the middle of the room where there sat a small table with a single Cold War-era telephone. He held his hand toward the phone and looked at us with the largest grin his face could contain. Then he said one word, "Call."

Leon and I looked at each other, then back at him.

"Call? Call who?" I asked.

His answer was simple, "Anyone," and shrugged. "Anywhere."

After two years in Albania, this was like magic. A secret phone, in the middle of nowhere, that I could use to call anyone and for free.

I dialed my parents. I couldn't believe it connected on the first try. "Mom. Mom. It's me. You are not going to believe where I am right now."

I wish talking to God was like that. I wish there was a magical means we had where we could just ring God up and he would pick up on the other end of the line. I would love to be able to chat with God about my day and hear about his. I think there would be so many things that I would like to talk to God about, if only there was some tangible evidence he was listening.

Why can't God talk to me like that?

God did talk to my friend Mollie like that once. She didn't even have to drive to a mountaintop military installation to do it either. Mollie talked to God in her car, while sitting in front of a Safeway. It happened last November.

Mollie is a tough girl, in many ways as rugged as those Albanian mountains. She is a single mom of a teenager. She is the girlfriend of a guy in a biker club. She has more than her share of tattoos and a romantic relationship with the color black. Mollie is my friend. Did I already say that?

Well, last November she was sitting in her car at the end of a horrible week. She was alone and was smoldering somewhere between rage and tears.

That is when God spoke. When she told me the story, she said, "It was as clear as the conversation we are having right now." God was comforting to her and wanted Mollie to know that he cared about her. She said, "I don't know how, but I just knew it was Jesus." That was strange because Mollie was not a Christian. She had never really landed in any religious camp. She had always had a faith that encompassed the whole world. It had never occurred to her that God might have a name, certainly not "Jesus."

Mollie said that they spoke for a few minutes. At the end she told God that she appreciated his attention and told "Jesus" that she would like to start to follow him, if that was all right.

"There is just one thing." Mollie stared at me to make sure that I was listening. "Jesus, there is one thing that I need from you. We are coming up on the end of the month here and I don't have a job. The bank account is pretty darn empty and I am not sure how I am going to feed my kid. God, if it is all the same to you, I need you to get me a job." And with that the dialogue ended. She said it like it was the most normal thing in the world.

The rest of her story went like this.

Hours later, Mollie was sitting on a friend's front porch. The scene could not have been more natural. Down the sidewalk and up to the porch walked a young woman, a relative of the house's owners. After some pleasantries, the woman looked at Mollie and asked, "Can you cook?"

"Sure. I have worked as a cook a few times in my life."

"Well," the lady said, "I need a cook for my café and I need one immediately. Any chance you need a job? Any chance you can start immediately?"

Why doesn't God talk to me that way?

You would think that during those missionary years God would have been breaking in left and right. Think about it, we were practically living out the book of Acts, the section of missionary stories from the Bible. We were living along the Mediterranean basin, just like the apostles and first churches of the New Testament. If I flip to the back of my Bible to the missionary maps (which look an awful lot like buccaneer maps, by the way), you might even find Illyricum (Albania's ancient name) listed along the Adriatic Sea. The apostle Paul said, "From Jerusalem all the way around to Illyricum, I have fully proclaimed the gospel of Christ."[1] Shouldn't we have been experiencing the God-appearance-filled life, like all those missionaries in the book of Acts?

Well, here is the thing about the book of Acts. The God appearances start to dry up before they ever get near Illyricum. Think about it: chapter 1, Jesus gets lifted into heaven. Which is, if I do say so myself, very cool. Chapter 2, we have Pentecost and the multicultural miracle of languages. Three, the healing of the beggar. In five, God kills Ananias and Sapphira. Gruesome. God's glory pours down on Stephen in chapter 7. Philip gets divine teleportation in eight. In chapter 9, God talks directly to Paul and personally converts him (talk about special attention). Cornelius's vision is in chapter 10, and then, well, it starts to thin out. Not completely, but it certainly starts to thin. Through the last eighteen chapters, there are a just few more miracles: a Macedonian vision and a direct communication from the Lord in chapter 23. Besides that, it is pretty human-centric stuff.

Through the rest of the New Testament, the God-encounters are very few as well, at least up until the end and John's vision of Jesus on the island of Patmos, which gives us the last book, appropriately titled "Revelation."

Some might read these last few paragraphs and feel that I am being critical of the Bible and its contents. I want to assure you I am not. I want to point out that it can be a great comfort to know that even in the Bible, the God-encounters are not popping up every other day.

I heard a Bible scholar once say: Many want to think of the Bible as a document full of God appearances. Some even want to call it a "book of miracles." Let me give you something to chew on. The most conservative estimates say it took more than 1,600 years to write the Bible. That is a huge stretch of time and included an untold number of generations. Of all those generations, there are really only three times in the Bible where we can responsibly say that supernatural events were normative: the events surrounding Moses's life, the events surrounding Elijah and Elisha's lives, and the time surrounding Jesus' last three years and the book of Acts. It is not that God-fireworks never happened in other places, they certainly did, but in those other times it could not be accurately considered normative.

Additionally, the four hundred years between the Old Testament and the New is called "The Great Silence." Four hundred years is a long time to wait, and heck, I get cranky when a church service seems dry.

This doesn't explain why God chooses to not interact with us more tangibly, but you know what? Sometimes it is nice to remember that we are not alone. Many, many people have gone through the fitful silence before us, and if you look at the names, we are in tremendously distinguished company.

———

I had a chance to meet Mother Teresa when I was living in Albania. It was a brief but private interaction, lasting no more than five minutes. It is one of the great treasures of my life. She was sublime and generous toward me, exactly what you might expect.

There are few people that exemplify the Jesus-Way more than that lovely, diminutive nun.

Mother Teresa once wrote to the Rev. Michael van der Peet:

Jesus has a very special love for you. As for me,
the silence and the emptiness is so great that I
look and do not see, listen and do not hear.

Those are some searing words, particularly coming from one of the great saints of her generation.

Reading her thoughts, it appears that I am not alone in the way that I feel. Not only am I not alone; I have the richest of company.

FIFTEEN
TRAVELING MERCIES

Not all who wander are lost.
—J. R. R. TOLKIEN

THROUGHOUT THOSE "IN THE world" adventures, circumstances and coincidences were breaking our way from time to time. If I could bring my mission-mates together in one room, we could prattle for days with the stories of spiritual surprise. We would tell tales of circumstantial luck: midnight rescues, emergency funding, simultaneous epiphanies, avoided arrests, dangers averted, and unexpected appointments.

Here are a few travel tales that have found a place in my memory museum.

IMMIGRATION POLICY

Our work created many opportunities for travel. Some of the time we were traveling to what you might call "difficult-access countries." Because of deliberating economics, political unrest, or religious oppression, many of our travels required special planning and some-times, cunning.

One time while in transit, my teammate Nikki lost her passport. It was the sort of oversight that could have happened to any of us. I actually thought it was a bit funny because Nikki is so astute and responsible. I, on the other hand, was the fool of our troupe. I once lost my passport while traveling and almost held up an entire excursion, but I had had the good fortune to do my bungling in northern Greece, a land with accessible American consulate services. Nikki was not so lucky.

She lost her passport in a forgotten corner of a country that was barely holding itself together at the time in all three realms: economic, political, and religious. She tore her suitcase apart looking for the missing documents, but to no avail. Identification thieves were a constant danger in these areas of the world, so we assumed she had been robbed. But a missing passport left us with a difficult decision.

There were ten of us and we were on a bit of a deadline. We had to get out of the country as quickly as possible, but the capitol was far off our path. Even if we could get to a "real city," we didn't know how extensive the consulate services would be.

Instead, we chose to forgo the long trip to the capitol and embrace a more adventurous plan. We decided to try and sneak Nikki across the border. Okay, okay, it may not have been the most brilliant idea, but we were young and well . . . young.

Luckily we were near a little-used border crossing where the military guards were not—how do I put this? Let's just say that their names were not on the short list to guard the palace.

We stuffed all ten of us into one vehicle and placed Nikki in the back row, center. We drove up into the mountains and came to the little-serviced crossing. When we arrived, we all stayed in our seats and let the guard come to us. There was a fair amount of perspiration at this point, and we were not sparing with our prayers.

When the uniformed soldier came to our window, rifle on his

shoulder and sidearm on his hip, he asked for our passports. The driver had them all ready, haphazardly stacked in no particular order. The officer looked around the interior of the car and then began to organize the passports. Our hope was that he would casually look them over and then wave us "good, clean, trustworthy Americans" through.

He did not.

Overseas, we learned the "two-foot square of the planet principle." We learned it from policemen and we learned it from black market moneychangers. Here is how the principle works. Everybody wants to be the ruler of something, even if it is just a two-foot square parcel of the planet. They rule that square with absolute autocratic power, and they will not release you from their two-foot domain until they feel you have acknowledged that power.

The border guard took each passport and fastidiously reviewed its contents. Then he would do his best to pronounce the individual's name (he had a dandy time with Kriz). Once the owner of the passport was identified, he would look intently at the person's face, then back at the picture in the passport, then back at the face, and then back at the passport. This went on until he felt satisfied that the identity was authentic. Only then would he move on to the next document. It was an excruciating process, and the temperature in the vehicle was rapidly rising. The perspiration and prayers increased with each passport.

When he reached the bottom of the stack, his face showed consternation. It was clear that he didn't know why, but something was amiss. He scoped the car's interior again, cataloguing each face. Then he took the stack of blue documents and started to count them.

We looked back and forth at one another and realized, *the gig is up.*

Just then, there was a shout from the guardhouse. The soldier shouted impatiently in response while trying to keep his count. The shouting grew. Frustrated, he turned to walk back, the passports fanned out in his hand.

We could not hear the exchange inside the building, but our soldier returned as anxious as a child who has just been scolded (perhaps he had encountered someone else's two-foot square). He took the stack of documents and began his process again, but before he could finish the first name, he thought better of it. Instead he stamped the immigration mark impatiently on each passport and handed the stack back with one hand while simultaneously barking at another soldier to open the gate.

We made it. All of us.

Quite a coincidence, wasn't it? But was it God? It was all so timely, even in our foolishness. If not for that shout from the guardhouse, I am sure that our day would have taken a substantive turn for the worse. Did God dip his finger into the scene to stir things up and save us?

While you are thinking about that, keep in mind that we were breaking the law. We were breaking both the country's law and international law. Is that something that God gets behind? Maybe only Nikki would have gone to jail, but all of us were smuggling an illegal and undocumented immigrant.

ANGELS UNAWARE

My buddy Todd and I were plane, train, and automobiling our way across Europe. We needed to get from Albania to England to pick up a Land Rover for the village work we were starting in the Albanian frontier. That's right, our task was to pick up a twelve-seat Land Rover in England and drive it from one corner of Europe to the other. I have had some seriously great jobs in my life.

This was my first extended foray into western Europe. We managed to Eurail our way as far as Munich. While there we met Maggie. She was a total sweetheart: a nurse with impeccable English who offered to be our guide as far as Paris. "I love Paris," she said. "Let me take a couple of days off, and I will be your personal tour guide around the city. Oh, and I have friends who can put us up, so we can afford the trip." For financial reasons we may have avoided Paris, but with Maggie as our guide, how could we go wrong? We could not have been better cared for if Gabriel himself had descended to our aid.

Maggie called her friend in Paris and confirmed we could stay with him. Then we were off to the rail station. We took a night train and arrived in Paris just as the sun was rising. We stashed our gear in a locker at the station near Sacre-Coeur and headed out to an unbelievable day of museums and monuments.

Periodically throughout the day, we would stop at a payphone to call Maggie's friend. He was proving difficult to get a hold of. "I am sure he is just busy," Maggie insisted.

The day passed, then the evening came and went. We had managed to keep to our meager budget, but the hours were ticking by. Sometime after midnight, we decided to head back to the train station. Maggie was getting worried about her friend, and we were all concerned about whether we were going to have a place to sleep. The most inexpensive hotel we could imagine in Paris was way beyond our means.

In the deserted station, Maggie headed out to find a phone to try and call again. Todd and I wandered around the massive space. *You could park New Jersey in here.*

In the cavernous silence, I heard one of the heavy glass doors open. A simple man with a bicycle shuffled through. The light was dim. I strained to watch him, walking toward me. The bike's derailleur hummed softly, and his feet *shooshed* across the tiled floor. He passed no more than fifteen feet away from me, so I said, "Hello." The man didn't speak at first, but instead turned the bike and came over to me.

When he got to my side, he returned my hello, and he asked, "What are you doing here?"

"We are trying to contact our friend," I said. "My name is Tony."

"I am Philippe. It is nice to meet you."

Philippe and I chatted for only maybe three minutes. He wished us luck and turned his bike to walk the final two hundred meters across the station's platform, his bike humming by his side.

A minute or so later, Maggie returned. Todd was with her now. She was noticeably upset. "What is it?"

"My friend changed his mind. He just changed his mind. He doesn't want guests. He says he is too tired. I don't know what to say, I am so sorry."

"What are we going to do?" Todd asked.

"I have absolutely no idea." She confessed with a shrug.

At this and without thinking, I wheeled around and yelled into the echoing darkness. "Philippe!" His name bounced around the massive space like a jai alai ball.

He was little more than a smudge in the darkness at the platform's far end, but I could tell he turned his bike and started the trek back.

I ran to him and when I got there, awkwardly stated, "We need your help. We have no place to stay. Do you know of an affordable hotel near here?"

Philippe thought for only a moment and then said, "Follow me."

We grabbed up our gear and trailed after, out the glass doors. We followed him up the boulevard, down a side street, down a smaller street, and stopped at a row-house hotel in the middle of the block. The four of us filled the small lobby. Philippe spoke quickly with the man behind the counter.

After just a couple minutes, he turned and said, "This man will take care of you."

The price for the night was something like twelve dollars US, and the room was lovely, quaint, and pristine.

As we gathered up our things and before I took a step to follow the manager up the stairs, I turned to talk to Philippe.

He was gone.

Do you believe in angels?

I think I do. I also think that sometimes they show up in these unusual and inexplicable ways.

Some people are quick to chalk a story like this up to coincidence: just a nice Frenchman (the only person around), who happened to be compassionate toward American tourists, with the right information, in the right place, in the middle of the night.

Others will have no problem calling this an angelic encounter.

Consider this. One other even more serendipitous encounter happened when I first journeyed into the country of Macedonia to spy out this new ministry location. The bus ride I took was long and uncomfortable. A fellow traveler made conversation time and again along the way, and when we arrived at the bus station in the Macedonian capitol, he asked me what I needed to do.

I numbered off a long list of tasks, each of which I had no idea how to complete. I didn't have a friend in the entire city. The man immediately offered to solve all my needs. He cancelled his entire day, and over the next five hours we completed each item on my list, a feat that would have taken me weeks alone. He seemed to know the perfect location to solve every problem, in a country that, at the time, did not take kindly to Protestant missionaries.

Was this an angel? If not an angel, was he God's divine provision just the same? The perfect person in the perfect place at the perfect moment?

Now, before you answer, there is one more detail I want to share. This chance-friend on the Macedonian bus had, let's just say, a colorful relationship with the English language. He did not speak a sentence that did not contain the most creative applications of my language's particularly potent profanities. Does the fact that he had a "potty mouth" change your view? Could God speak through a profane vessel?

MILOSEVIC

One time, my duties required me to travel to Budapest, Hungary, for meetings. For whatever reason, I didn't want to splurge on the plane ticket. The train was much less expensive. There was just one problem. The train route required that I travel across Serbia from the southern border all the way through the north.

It gets worse. At the time, US warplanes were bombing the snot out of Serbian troops in Kosovo. The Serbs were slaughtering Albanian-Kosovar civilians by the thousands. Entire villages were being eradicated. Trails of Kosovar poor were walking unbelievable distances across the mountains into Albania just to survive: the elderly, the very young, the sick. This crisis was unimaginable.

Because of the bombing, Americans were caustically hated by the Serbian government. Under no circumstance was an American passport to be allowed across Serbia's borders.

But I didn't care. I chose to dare fate. Even though the route crossed Serbia, I bought a ticket anyway and tried my luck.

When we arrived at the Serbian border, I was forcibly dragged from the train by soldiers and, in broken English, told that I would not be allowed to enter. This was expected, but I knew that this was only the first round.

I wandered around the train platform for a while. In time I figured out the train officer with the highest rank. I introduced myself to him. I made no effort to communicate in anything but English, passing myself off as an ignorant American traveler. I insisted that I just wanted to get to Hungary.

The man huffed at me. I thanked him for listening and then took a seat conspicuously on a bench where he couldn't ignore me and waited.

Over the next few hours, I just sat. The officer kept looking over at me, and his glances became increasingly consternate.

Eventually, I think he concluded that I was simply a fool and a fool that he didn't want to deal with any longer.

Just as a train prepared to pull out, he grabbed me by the strap of my backpack and shoved me through the door of a passenger car before my documents could be checked. He was done with me. I would be someone else's fool to deal with.

I found a seat next to the window and kept my head down. Half an hour in, I showed my ticket to the conductor without making eye contact or speaking. Up through Serbia we traveled.

A few hours later, we crossed into the capitol city, Belgrade.

Signs of the dictatorial Milosevic regime were everywhere. I found myself daydreaming. My mind was full of thoughts of Kosovars. Like a Holocaust documentary, pictures of wholesale murders and mass graves filled my mental movie screen. I thought about Serbia's leader, Slobodan Milosevic, who was, at that very moment, probably within a few miles of my slowly moving train car. A few years later this dictator would be tried as a war criminal under the crime of genocide. But today, he was free, an instrument of unspeakable murderous violence. My hatred seethed inside me.

That was when my imaginings plummeted. My fists balled in my lap as I thought of how I would kill him if I ever had the chance. I daydreamed of plunging a knife into his neck; the euphoric feeling of his flesh splitting open. I imagined the slight vibration in the handle as the blade scratched against the vertebrae of his spine. I could feel the coarse scraping as I sawed through his windpipe and vital veins. I felt the blood squirting on my face, and I reveled in his howling turned to gurgling as he drowned in his own blood, the splattering coughs from his mouth and open throat.

If an idiot like me can sneak across the border on a train, how much harder would it be to get close enough to at least get a clear shot at this monster? No one had checked my bag. I could have come with any one of a number of tools of death.

I started to ask God if he wanted me to do it. *Lord, my Bible is full of your assassinations. There is righteous killing all over my Old Testament. Maybe now is a time for you to put this particular part of your divine will to good use. Dietrich Bonhoeffer plotted to kill Hitler; are my desires any less righteous? Let me kill him. Please.*

This experience brought my ugliness to bear. I wanted to kill. I was not driven by righteousness or the good of the world. My motivation was anger. My inspiration was retribution.

I don't have the pay grade to know what God sees as righteous in this world of violence, murder, and atrocity. If nothing else, I was now more sure than ever that I have no place on the jury of humanity.

My heart is so sick, filled with prejudices, judgment, and abuses. Jesus equated spiritual wholeness to "love your enemy" and "pray for your enemy." It never even crossed my mind to pray for Milosevic. Nothing in me wanted God's grace for him. What is the good of our gospel if it does not have space for even the worst among us? What hope is there for my vile heart?

In light of these things, I must consider the possibility: Maybe God doesn't speak to me because I am just not ready for it. Maybe God is protecting me because he knows just the sort of brutality I might ask for.

SIXTEEN
THE CALL

*I don't always know the right thing to do, Lord; but I think
that the fact that I want to please you, pleases you.*
—THOMAS MERTON

IF WE ARE HONEST, I think most of the time we are content in God's silence. It is not anything against God, we are just used to taking care of stuff on our own, without the distraction of God's agenda. Do I really need God to help me mow my lawn, balance my checkbook, or drive my kids to soccer practice? Additionally, an ever-awareness of God can really cramp my style. I don't want to think about the starving poor when I am trying to choose which cut of beef to buy for our backyard barbecue. I don't want to think of people dying on the world's other side (often with cheaply curable diseases) when I am meeting with my financial planner. I don't want to think about the hurting people I pass everyday from the protective safety of my car. If I start having God-awareness all the time, I might have to think about those sorts of God-priorities, and that would be a real bummer.

There are, however, the *other* times, the times when the longing for God's presence does make its way onto my agenda. These are the times when I am desperate for help, need comfort, or am begging for wisdom. These moments shatter my habits of pragmatism and body check me from my self-reliance.

That was certainly true when my sister called me from Cincinnati.

It had been about a year since Ransom was first diagnosed, a year of unknown, a year of desperation, and a year of his mother (my sister) crying out to God. Ransom's drawn-out treatment had led them to Cincinnati in hopes of finding new healing options. It started out a great trip. In fact, it was a wonderfully hopeful season. Against all odds, Ransom was showing some really positive signs. And when they first arrived at the Ohio hospital, the optimism only grew.

At first they had not been able to get access to the main oncologists, but the hospital's support staff had performed a number of tests and those tests had produced the most encouraging results. In fact, it looked like the chemo might be winning the war on Ransom's tumors.

Hope can lift one off the ground like a hot air balloon.

Well, when the oncologists finally arrived a few days later, the story radically reversed. Their assessment of Ransom's condition shot a ballistic missile through my sister's hope-balloon.

Before I continue, you need to know a few things about my sister. When God was dealing out our family genetics, I got all the drama genes. My sister is the rock. She is polite, wise, appropriate, caring, demure, measured, and calm. She is a pillar of strength (while I tend toward a status more aptly titled: "Bobo, the monkey boy"). These pillar-like qualities set the expectations for this particular story.

I will never forget the day of that phone call, the day her hope-balloon exploded. I was standing on the thin strip of grass along the street in front of my house. We had only been on the phone for a minute. My sister was seething through the receiver, acid was leaking into my ear. "I am so angry at God." When she said the word "angry," her voice went low and quivered. "I am so angry." Then she slipped into a rolling sob. I sat silently with her, a helpless companion in her sorrow. Together we thought only of Ransom.

I remember getting off the phone and standing there staring up into the sky. I had no idea what to do, but there was one thing that I was positively sure of that day: My sister knows God. She knows him. There is simply no doubt, and her visceral emotions proved it.

Sure, it is possible to be angry at someone you don't have a personal connection with. We may get disturbed, even chagrinned, by people we have no direct connection to (politicians, people in the news, figures from history). But the lion's share of my most intense anger is always saved for people I actually know or who have hurt someone that I actually know (just ask my best friends or my wife). When we are relationally connected, the pain gets real. It gets visceral.

My sister's pain was visceral because my sister knows God.

I don't understand people who say they have never been angry at God. I don't get it. They have never yelled at the sky, shaken their fist in the air, or told God to "go to hell." They have never quietly seethed under a blanket of tears. It makes me wonder if they have ever *really* talked to God at all.

After my sister said good-bye (as best she could), I stood next to the road in front of my house for several minutes. I begged God to be present in my sister's pain. I begged him to respond to her faith, as messy and angry as it was. *Visit her, please,* was my prayer.

———

Flying and falling feel the same until they reach their destination.

Another time that we long for God to show up is when we need life-clarifying wisdom. At least that has been true in my story. One of those times was in the fall of 1996.

I had returned to the States. It was supposed to be a respite, a time of rest, recovery, and preparation, but I couldn't rest. I am not even sure I had the capacity to rest. I couldn't wait to throw myself back into the breach.

I was solely focused on getting back into the world. I was desperate for my next assignment. I did not, however, know that it would be my final assignment overseas. At the time, I fully believed that I would live the whole of my life jumping from location to location across the globe. I thought it was my destiny, still tragically unaware of my desperate race to get God to notice me.

Well, it turned out that my desperate race would not last much longer. Though the end was still a couple years out, the fuse was burning.

I had already made several short-term trips to the country of Macedonia. I had been tasked with preparing the site for new missionary work. Everything was in place for the first teams, and I believed that I was ready to take on an elevated role in that new frontier.

For now, I was back home in Oregon. My heart was already pointed toward Macedonia, but I didn't want to treat the decision process casually. It was quite possibly the most substantive verdict of my young life. It was not just the next place on my map; it was a change of status. No longer would I be just a "hired gun" for my missionary agency; I would be a long-term imbedded missionary. It was the sort of step that might finally get me noticed.

First I needed to confirm my calling. That is how the system works. I needed some sort of spiritual pixie dust to confirm Macedonia as my destination. Everybody in the religious world knows, "It is not enough to *want* to do something; you must be *called* to it." So I needed a little divine mojo to seal the deal, for my internal justification but even more importantly so I would have something to tell others when they asked me how I knew I was called to go.

So I headed to a cabin in the Cascade Mountains to find God. I needed his voice and I needed his leading (or at least his confirmation of the decision I had already made). I spent several days in prayer, fasting and "seeking God's face." It seemed like the right thing to do.

It was the sort of retreat that I had been taught wins God's favor, and if God is gracious, could result in his voice.

Even in my fasting and focused prayer, I still had no idea the toll that my fatal flaw had taken on my soul. Like a cheese grater within me, my insides were already frayed and fragile, but I couldn't see it. I refused to see it. I had not yet done close to enough to earn God's attention. In my insanity, I needed to increase the velocity of my life, not slow it down.

As a part of my retreat meditation, I chose to read the book of Acts. What better choice could there be than to seek God's voice in a book about the earliest missionary trips by the Christian church? Paul, Peter, and Stephen would be perfect guides. Surely God would not deny my plea for wisdom.

On the second day of my mediation, I came to chapter 16 and read:

> They passed through the Phrygian and Galatian region, having been forbidden by the Holy Spirit to speak the word in Asia; and after they came to Mysia, they were trying to go into Bithynia, and the Spirit of Jesus did not permit them; and passing by Mysia, they came down to Troas. A vision appeared to Paul in the night: *a man of Macedonia was standing and appealing to him, and saying, "Come over to Macedonia and help us."* When he had seen the vision, immediately we sought to go into Macedonia, concluding that God had called us to preach the gospel to them.[1]

There it was. There it was! Certainly, I had read this passage many times before. I had probably even taught it as an example of Christian decision-making, teaching things like: "Notice how God closed the doors for the apostles to go to Asia or to Mysia. Always be aware of God's open doors."

However, on that day, in that cabin, with my stomach empty and my heart searching, the story of the apostle Paul became *my* story.

It was written for me, "Come over to Macedonia and help us." Did it matter that the passage probably referred to the Macedonians of Greece and I wanted to go to Slavic Macedonians (a completely different people group)? Of course not. God was using the words of my Bible to speak to me loud and clear. His will was that I fulfill *my* plan and go to Macedonia as his emissary, just as Paul had.

The double bonus was that Paul was clearly a guy who God did not ignore. Could I hope for the same?

It doesn't take a genius to hear the tone of this story. You have probably already guessed that this tale is not going to end well. If you have the courage and interest to keep reading, you will find out the rest of the story. But before we go there, I want to share something with you. That fasting retreat in the Cascade Mountains was a crystallized example of my twisted waltz with God.

I love God, I really do. I want God to lead me. However, I so want to believe that God is with me that I must confess my capacity to conjure his presence for my own comfort or control. I must acknowledge my ability to co-opt for my agendas and to defend my opinions. To adapt Jean-Jacques Rousseau's famous words: God created us in his own image, and it is amazing how often I return the favor.

Years later, after the chaos of my life had taken its toll, I can remember looking back on that mountain retreat, and all I could feel was disdain. How many people had I told about the moment God spoke to me though Acts 16? How many times had I used this story to justify my "calling" to Macedonia and to prove to others that I was the sort of person God talks to? I had used it to prove I was on God's team, only to discover that I was more doubting Thomas than apostle Paul.

It made me sick. I had heard what I wanted to hear, nothing more. For years, I believed that I had just propped up a cardboard cutout God and put my own words inside his mouth.

But that was then.

Now, many years have passed. I am in my forties and quietly

living in Portland, Oregon. With the passing of the decades, another perspective has birthed. This new perspective does not replace my self-critique. I am still convinced that my decisions in that mountain cabin were selfish, even fueled by my pathologies. I believe I saw what I wanted to see in the pages of my Bible, nothing more. In fact, my choices may have been so delusional that I had actually chosen to read the book of Acts, not for inspiration, but because I knew it would lead me to chapter 16 and my justification through the "Macedonian call." It might have all been my own insidious setup. But, ultimately that is only one side of the story.

There is another narrative to this discussion. Instead of always being so darn self-oriented, how might this scenario look from God's perspective? Does my insidiousness hinder God's leading? Do I have that much power? Is God thwarted by my mixed motives and spiritual manipulations? Now, as I prayerfully reflect on my past, I think God was in fact fully vested in my plan in that mountain cabin. Today, I have come full circle and believe God *was* actually present in that circumstance. I believe that there was work that God *needed* to do in me. He was fully committed to that work, and that work may have required my chaos to fully run its course. Maybe God is just the sort of Being to lead us through our pathologies just as effectively as through "godly" things like the Bible.

And that may be the greatest mercy of all.

Reanimation by Jonathan Case

PART 4
REANIMATION

THERE IS A SAYING: "Superheroes never die...they just wait to be reborn in a new series or a parallel universe." Death and rebirth are constant themes for both the superhero and normal human experience.

Get busy being born or get busy dying.

—BOB DYLAN

SEVENTEEN
THE M-WORD

I'm so scared I'm holding my breath
While You're up there just playing hard to get . . .
I can't see how You're leading me unless You've led me here
Where I'm lost enough to let myself be led
And so You've been here all along, I guess
It's just Your ways, and You are just plain hard to get
—"HARD TO GET," RICH MULLINS

A HARVEST IS A violent thing.

Sure, months later, when the barn is stocked and bellies are full, a harvest feels like a wonderful gift. But the act of harvesting is unapologetic, cold, and emotionless violence. Living things are sliced and ripped and screechingly uprooted. I suppose that is why the Angel of Death carries a scythe, because from the perspective of the ground and grass, harvest is nothing more than a circus of death.

You are God's field.

—1 CORINTHIANS 3:9 NASB

Jesus once composed a story of a thief who planted tares (weeds) among a wheat field. The workers in the field wanted to pull up the choking plants, but the field owner told them to wait. The tares and the wheat were far too interlaced. The two could not be separated. He assured the workers that when the time was right, he would rip the tares and the wheat out together. It would be violent.

In this last season of my twenty-something missionary journeys, the false beliefs from my fatal flaws had grown to maturity in my soul. They had twisted themselves so indivisibly around my Jesus-beliefs that I could no longer tell them apart. Just like in another of Jesus' field stories, these tare-beliefs were choking out my faith.

My "call" to Macedonia finally came to fruition. In my seemingly limitless foolishness, I moved to Macedonia without a long-term team. The plan was for me to coordinate a series of short-term teams until more permanent partners could be found. At the time, Macedonia was not exactly the scariest ministry location on the planet, but it did have real challenges. Its government ruled from the shadows and was mostly ignored by the rest of the world. They wielded laws that the rest of Europe should have summarily condemned. For instance, they had an undeniable malevolence for foreign missionaries, so much so that random arrests and interrogations were commonplace. In fact, during that first year I was there, government police forcibly deported one quarter of the missionaries in Macedonia. Suffice it to say, it behooved us to keep a low profile.

The stress of those security issues got thrown into the caldron with my messiah complex, my aching loneliness, my desperation to get God to notice me, my frayed soul, and my penchant for seven-day workweeks. The resulting poison is self-evident.

A few months after my move, my soul finally passed out. I don't think it was dead, but it certainly no longer showed signs of life. I had always been a disciplined kid, even from those early childhood years. Rising early for long sessions of Bible reading and prayer had marked most every morning for decades. In Macedonia it was the same. I would rise early, often before six, make a cup of coffee, and return to my room for my time of study, yet my unconscious soul made it impossible. I would stare at my Bible. It was nothing but mush. Sometimes I would read out loud to try and wake my soul, but it was hopeless. I couldn't piece the verses together, and I had no idea how any of them applied to real life.

Eventually, I gave up Bible reading all together. It was a vacancy. Instead, I started just kneeling next to my bed like a child. Quiet and numb, I would try to pray, but the only words I could muster were, "I choose to believe you exist today. I choose to believe you exist today. I choose to believe you exist today. I choose to believe you exist today." On and on like this I would chant, sometimes for over an hour. No prayers for my family or friends. No prayers for the beautiful short-termers in Macedonia, who I was supposed to be caring for. No prayers for the people of Macedonia or the world, just "I choose to believe you exist today."

I wish I could say that it stopped there, but it didn't. My passed-out soul emitted vile toxins. Anger, manipulation, and chaos became harder and harder to stifle away. Some days I was able to manufacture normalcy, but those days were often replaced by madness.

I was clinging and clawing for help. I came to lean on those precious short-termers, fresh out of college. One lady in particular captured my heart. I relied on her friendship. I clung to her like a drowning child to keep me from falling apart, but how can any person hold together another's dying soul?

I steeped in this sorry state for more than a year. All the while, as they say, the ministry must go on. I did my best to hold it together, and the long days stacked one upon the other.

One day, in my second year, I was called to some regional meetings in Budapest. This may have even been that same trip when I snuck across Serbia and "plotted" the assassination of Milosevic. I'm not sure; it is all quite fuzzy to me now. If it was, I now see that my murderous desires toward the Serbian dictator may have been little more than an extension of my self-loathing.

While in Budapest, between meetings, I tried to explain to my leadership that I was struggling. I told them that I needed substantive relief. We managed to negotiate a reduction in my duties. When I got back to Macedonia, I would focus on just language learning, long-term planning, security, and an ample dose of personal care. Weekly care of the short-term teams would be turned over to others. This strategy reduced my responsibilities by half. I hoped it would help me find some balance. Sadly, those reduced expectations never saw the light.

Little did I know, the wheels of my fate were already in motion.

I returned to Macedonia to find a small pastoral team that was visiting briefly from the States. There was one ministry leader and a couple of helpers. The current short-term team was about three months into their stint.

The care team found "crisis." It sounded to them like a fire truck siren: "Crisis! Crisis! Crisis!" The tensions were real and much of it was because of the emotional chaos I had unleashed over those previous months. Several team members had lodged complaints, but no one had been hurt worse than my dear lady-friend, the one I told you I had been leaning on so heavily for emotional support.

I ask you, is there a greater evidence of insanity than when our best attempts at love actually leave the other soul in pulsing pain and turmoil?

Ministry Leader called me out that very night to talk. He explained that the chaos was overwhelming and unacceptable. Over the next hours, he explained how it was my fault. Part of me wanted to explain. I wanted him to know that I hadn't touched anyone or wanted to hurt . . . but the truth was, people had depended on me, and I had left at least one dear soul in pain. So I offered no excuse.

He described me in vile and piercing words. I am not saying he was wrong; it was just simply the most gutting conversation of my life. His accusations amounted to declaring that, although I had not performed any specific wrongful acts, I was, nonetheless, an abusive person.

Back in the States, I later learned there was another term that was cycling throughout my ministry-tribe. The word was *molester*. That's right, *molester*. The word was modified with the word *relational*; I was a *relational molester*. Regardless of the modifier, once you let the *m*-word out of the bottle, you can never put it back. Over those next years, I would drag the *m*-word with me whereever I went. I would find myself searching faces in a crowd, wondering who else thought of me that way. Labels have a habit of sticking to the soul.

That night, I was fired. Ministry Leader told me to pack my things and get out of the country.

I returned to my apartment well after midnight. I spent those early morning hours standing in front of my second-story window and staring out at the lights of this city I had made my home. My eyes drifted slowly across Skopje's downtown, the bridges and the fortress ruins on top of the hill. I was not crying, at least not at this moment. It was more of an inaudible groan from deep inside me. My eyes were fixed on the now-silent city to which I had committed my life. *What had I done?*

The shame was staggering. *My life is over. It is simply over.* I had managed to flush a decade of work like so much excrement. No one would ever hire me again. Hire me? At that moment I could not believe that anyone would even want to look at my face again.

Within days my entire missionary family, in Albania and across Eastern Europe, would know of my insidious failure. Among the eyewitnesses of my demise was one of my sister's best friends, a person intimately connected to my ministry family back home, a member of my home church, and one of my longtime ministry apprentices. *Was there any sphere of my life that would not know the whole of my nauseating fall?*

There is certainly no place on the planet for someone like me.

I spent most of the night in front of that window. When morning light came, I started the process of packing my things.

I tell you this story not because I want to. Let me assure you, you now have more of the dark details than I would want anyone to know, even my closest friends. Everybody knows that I was fired from my job in Eastern Europe, and I have always made it clear that it was my fault, but the finality of the shame and words like *molester* have rarely been spoken by me before.

I have to tell you this story; I have to because you must know it if you are going to understand what happens next.

That same afternoon, I walked around the city with my dear and unfaltering mentor, Don Mansfield. He listened to me process my pain. He did not judge me, even though his reputation was also taking a beating because of my pathologies.

As the afternoon waned, he turned to me and, with his soft, compassionate eyes, offered me his one small piece of advice, "Tony, go home. Go to bed early. Sleep a long night and when you wake, spend the morning with Jesus."

I stared straight at him with my eyes wide and lips pursed. I tried to hold it in, but I couldn't. A hyena-laugh burst out. The thought was preposterous. He might as well invite me to flap my arms and fly around the city. "Spend the morning with Jesus." That is laughable.

It is safe to say I had officially lost it. I was drunk with depression and didn't care. I vomited my insanity all over my old friend.

He didn't blink. His face didn't move. When my chaos finally receded, he looked at me with righteous sobriety and said, "Listen to me. Go home. Go to bed early. Sleep a long night and when you wake, spend some time with Jesus."

I paused. I absorbed his council. His sober spirit infected me, and I surrendered to his faith.

I hugged him and turned to walk alone back to my apartment.

The next morning I awoke surprisingly refreshed. The emotional exhaustion had done its work. I had slept maybe ten hours. It was still early, before seven. I went to the kitchen to make my ritual cup of coffee. I sat watching the boiling grounds-filled water slide slowly through the red plastic funnel and paper filter, the bubbles slowly slipping to the surface with a murky pop.

Then, all at once, I remembered where I was. Reality rushed upon me: the shame, the names, the mistakes, the pain I had caused, the chaos I had created, the end of the only life I knew. The sobbing broke like a storm cloud. I could not contain the wails. I groped for the countertop to keep myself from buckling. *God, help me?*

After several minutes, when strength began to be restored, I slowly carried my pint-sized mug to my bedroom. I had to concentrate to keep the sobbing from leaking down to my hand. I managed to make it to my room without incident, and I placed the mug on my desk. I took my usual place at the end of my bed, near the curtained window, back against the wall.

I loved my little room, lined with my books and my wide desk. I loved my little bed, my feet dangling off the edge, with its soft blue-plaid down comforter. All this would be mine for only a couple more days. Soon it would be gone. I had thrown it all away.

Don had asked me to spend time with Jesus. God had ignored me for so long. *How do I even begin?* I took my Bible and opened to the Gospels. I knew that I could at least find Jesus there.

I tried to read, but the all-too-familiar confusion found me again.

I was lost, simply lost. My head rocked back and bounced against the plaster wall, and the sobs came again. I surrendered to them. I let them take me.

This is when something beyond explanation happened. It was the single most extraordinary moment of my aloof-journey with my elusive God.

Through the door of my room, only six feet away, walked Jesus.

Mock me if you will, but I have never been more sure of anything in my life. The presence was so strong that I felt it all around me. It was as if Jesus entered and physically sat down on the bed next to me, the springs bending under the added weight, and his arms wrapped firmly and reassuringly around me.

His invitation was simple: *read*.

Within moments, the words on the page, with the energy of a playground at morning recess, bounced and danced before me. We read together. We read from the Gospels and we read from the Psalms. Occasionally the tears returned, but they were different. Now, they were not rooted in shame.

Then we sang. I had forgotten what it felt like to sing a prayer and feel it within me like an anthem from a Broadway play.

That was it, the two of us together on the end of my bed: sustenance . . . comfort . . . satisfaction . . . belonging.

It was only hunger that eventually snatched me from my reverie. If you had asked me at that exact moment, I would have said that a couple of hours had come and gone.

I climbed off my bed and walked to the living room and only then realized the windows were darkened. It was not late morning or even afternoon. We were into the evening, and the light of dusk was the soft glow outside.

The whole day had been lost away. It was like nothing I had ever experienced before or since. It was my road to Emmaus. It was my still small voice at the cave of Mount Horeb. It was my lingering afternoon under the oaks of Mamre (which is another odd *m*-word). Some could argue that it was just insanity born from a cocktail of stress and rejection, but that is honestly not an option I am willing to consider. How can I? Even my ever-critical mind refuses to be cynical, having succumbed to that invading love.

It was my most crystalline moment of desperation, failure, and shame. It was in that sensation of bankruptcy that Jesus showed up. Maybe that is a glimpse of what Jesus meant when he said, "Blessed are the poor in spirit." I wonder then if my lack of true personal bankruptcy throughout the rest of my life might explain why God most often seems distant.

Whatever the trigger, it is my story's one precious, undeniable encounter with the Divine.

I wish I could tell you that everything was great after that. It was not. Quite the opposite, in fact. Jesus had given me only a way station, a place to rest, the grace to get me through that one single day.

The next day, the heavens were bronze again, but there remained a seed of hope, hope that I had not been wholly forgotten. I soon learned that the work of God had only been commissioned. It would not be easy work, nor would it be fast.

The next day, I rose early and began deciding to whom I would give my belongings. I had been forbidden to visit those people who had been under my charge just three days before. While fully acknowledging my insanity, I still loved them very much.

A few days later I left my "home" forever. My life as I knew it was over. Even in the chaos, I was strangely relieved. I was like a fugitive who had finally been caught. A captured man can finally sleep.

A harvest is a violent thing.

The tares of lies and destructive beliefs had grown to maturity and twisted themselves inseparably around my best beliefs of the Jesus-Way. The time had come to replant the fields in my soul, but there was no subtle or civilized solution to my sorry state.

My Uncle Larry, a six-foot-seven retired African American cop, says to me often, "God does not want to wound you. He wants you to die. Just die! Allow God to kill you, that he might live."

In my case, as a striving, mercenary-minded, actions-addicted, relentless runner who *also* wanted to follow God and desired true devotion, I was stuck. My beliefs had become irreconcilably intertwined. My wheat-belief in God as heavenly Father had been twisted by my tare-conviction that God wanted to push me away. My wheat-belief that I could participate with God's kingdom was twisted by my tare-paradigms of production and comparison.

What was I to do? The answer: there was nothing that I could do. I needed to die. God loved me enough to bring circumstance that would scrape the landscape of my soul clean and fallow. It was not atheism; it was belieflessness. It was time to start from scratch, a cleared field, marked by the stench of manure, but also with a frail hope for a fertile future.

If that fertile future were to come to pass, it would need to be replanted slowly . . . one belief at a time.

EIGHTEEN
FATHER TIME

But God remembered Noah...
—GENESIS 8:1[1]

I WAS WRESTED FROM Macedonia and relocated to Budapest, Hungary.

God had scraped my faith field clean, uprooting my toxic beliefs along with my godly ones. It was not unbelief. It was not belief. It was barrenness.

To use a modern metaphor, it was like my operating system had gone irrevocably bad, bogged down and compromised by a thousand bugs and viruses. At some point, if you want to save the machine, all you can do is scrape the hard drive clean and start over.

I have no doubt that God wanted to save me. I have no doubt that God released me to the chaos of my fatal flaws within that caldron of circumstance out of his severe mercy. Looking back now, it is one of the kindest things that anyone has ever done for me.

My missionary leadership pulled me from Macedonia and deposited me in Budapest. I was graciously provided a one-room guesthouse in which to sleep, and I was asked to wait while they deliberated the verdict on my fate. My presence was a nuisance, and I soon learned that it was more pragmatic to simply forget I was there. Have you ever been forgotten? Usually "forget" is a passive concept (I forgot that memory, I forgot to brush my teeth, I forgot where I put my keys), but other times, the painful times, it is intentional: my old church has forgotten about me; my ex-husband has forgotten about me; my dear buddy found new friends and forgot about me. It is the intentional "forgettings" that sear us.

One week turned to two. Then the weeks turned to months, and the months started to stack up. It became increasingly impossible for me to find ways to fill the seemingly endless hours of each day. Most days I spent wandering the streets alone. There are whole weeks, maybe even months that are just gaps in my memory. I was lost in a personal and spiritual vacancy.

I was sympathetic; my leadership was in an impossible position. They knew I had rotted right before them on the mission field. They doubted that I even believed the creed any longer. What are missions leaders to do with a missionary who can't believe? I am sure the pressure increased for them, fueled by the escalating language circulating about me back in the States.

Honestly, I think they probably wanted to fire me and be done with it. And I can hardly blame them. They had dozens of missions and thousands of workers to think about. A broken and worthless chump like me didn't deserve to be a priority. Ironically, though they may have wanted to fire me, they couldn't. I hadn't actually broken any policies: I hadn't gotten drunk or punched a subordinate. I hadn't embezzled funds or succumbed to lust. Try as they might, they were stuck with me.

So I sat. I was alone. Alone with my passed-out soul, my relational blight, and my bereaved heart. Most days I would ride to the center of Budapest and trudge about, waiting for the end of the day. Some afternoons, I would tire of walking and ride the circle tram around the city. The motion supplied ever-changing scenery. I would sit with my forehead against the thick glass. I could lose hours that way. That was all that hours were good for—to get lost.

We humans are funny creatures. We invent the most inexplicable ways to cope with the circumstances about us.

One of my odd coping mechanisms in this season of hurt was to buy stuff. I would stop and buy little things. I know that is strange, but it was true. Periodically, I would find myself wandering into a store and buying something that I absolutely didn't need or even want. My desk, for instance, had a stack of CDs that I had never even listened to. They sat unopened. How many Vangelis or *Best of the Bangles* CDs does one person need? (Well, actually, I loved my Bangles CD.)

I have a hypothesis as to why I bought these things. I believe there was something about the act of buying that helped me feel not so alone, if only for a moment. I would select an item and go to the counter. I would give the clerk my money and they would give me my object, and for just an instant, one fleeting moment, we would connect through exchange. It may not seem like much, but a drop of water feels different when you are crawling through a desert.

On a broader level, I wonder if this explains part of the insidious power of consumerism.

On one of my endless Budapest afternoons, I was riding again on the circle tram. From my seat, mid-car, my head against the glass, I faintly watched the world go by. There were cars and shops and churches and telescoping boulevards like the spokes of a wheel.

With no particular provocation, at an unexceptional stop, I pulled myself from my seat and out onto the street. I walked slowly down the sidewalk under the building overhang, the sounds of the city bouncing off my head. A block down, I came to a bookstore. What use did I have with a Hungarian bookstore? None, but I went in anyway. It was like I was living out a Monty Python sketch: have you ever seen "The Depressed Traveler in a Hungarian Bookstore" sketch?

I opened the heavy glass door and wandered to the shop's center. Spinning around me, above the shelves, were placards covered in odd words. Hungarian is the sort of language where polyglots go to die: awkward letter combinations and an impossible syntax. I didn't have the bandwidth to learn more than a dozen words.

I was about to turn back to the street when, in the back corner, my mind caught words that it recognized. Barely more conscious than a coma, I wandered back to find a shelf of English books.

In keeping with my consumerist coping mechanism, and without reading the titles, I lifted my hand up, just above eye level and to my left. A narrow red binding caught my eye, and I slid it from its place. Without looking at it, I walked hypnotically to the clerk's counter for my hit of relational exchange.

When my turn came, I stepped to the counter.

I mustered a smile and so did she.

I gave her the red book and my currency. She took them. She made change from the till and placed the foreign coins in the palm of my hand. She then slid my red book into a bag. I absorbed her every movement. I wanted her to take as long as possible. I watched her make sure the book sat at the bag's very center. She carefully closed the bag's top with a crease, and with just her fingertips handed the bag to me with a thank you. Then she dismissed me by looking past me to her next sale.

The moment was gone and I was alone again.

Out the glass door I went. I wandered down a few shops to find an Elizabethan teahouse. It was decorated in ornate oversized moldings with lemon walls and heavy tile flooring. I slipped as anonymously as possible to the shop's rear and took a seat at the empty table in the far back corner.

A few minutes later, a lady brought me a cup of tea. At first I didn't touch it. I watched the shy steam float on the liquid's surface and then rise in a string and twirl in the air before me.

On the corner of the table sat the bag from the bookstore, the size and shape of the book barely discernable through the paper.

I slipped my hand inside and removed the book. I moved the teacup to the side and placed the red cover faceup in front of me on the table. It confused me. The spark plugs in my brain were not firing correctly, so the book registered slowly.

There was a dark painting in the cover's middle, and the lettering was in gold. The author, I later learned, was a Catholic priest and a spiritual guide to many. His name was Henri Nouwen, and the book I had randomly selected was called *The Return of the Prodigal Son*.

The Return of the Prodigal Son is an exploration of Jesus' famous story (found in Luke 15) of a son who ran recklessly out into the world, far from his father. Later, after being submerged in shame and only after total personal, emotional, and spiritual bankruptcy, he returned to his father's presence, not believing that the father-son relationship was even possible.

Through the pages of the red book, Henri Nouwen meditates through this very story. He does so with the Dutch painter Rembrandt, who famously painted the moment of the prodigal son's return to his love-stricken father. It was Rembrandt's painting that resided on the red book's cover, and it provided a second text for Nouwen's musings.

This is how God chose to slowly start to replant the fields of my faith. He planted one belief at a time. The first seeds God chose were a freshly formed understanding of father.

That first year, God's only agenda was fatherhood, specifically the fatherhood of God. The first portal of his replanting was a red bound book from an inconspicuous Hungarian bookstore.

It is significant to me now that God chose to begin with this intimate picture of the Divine. We could have started with God as Creator, God as holy, God as Great Spirit, or any other pictures from the divine mountain, but instead I was given a loving and present parent. If the agenda had come from within me (like in the Cascade mountaintop cabin in chapter 16), the topic would have been God as mission, God as activist or God as world changer, but no . . . instead it was a particularly quiet image of family.

I spent the next weeks with Nouwen and Rembrandt. The pages moved like a glacier. I had to read each sentence three or more times to even begin to understand them. It was not that the words were that complicated; it was just that my soul had atrophied so extensively that spiritual language was as foreign to me as Hungarian.

The book, the painting, and my quiet reflections dug deeper and deeper inside me, one shovelful at a time.

The most unshakable epiphany during this time was the idea of stillness. In the Rembrandt painting, the father is standing near the painting's center and his prodigal son is kneeling on the ground before him. The son is haggard, broken, and bankrupt. His head is shaved and his clothes are soiled and frayed. The young man's head is pressed against his father's belly like a young child. The father is old. His body is a bent shelter over the child-man before him. His hands rest ever so compassionately and securely on his son's shoulders and back.

Now here is the epiphany: neither of them wanted to leave, or even move. The father was as still as a sequoia and just as present. *Being* was the only agenda. In the painting, it is as if the figures had been there together for a long, long time, and there was zero indication that either had the slightest intention of moving. The stillness—their stillness—was the shocking thing to me.

Early in Rembrandt's life, he had composed another rendition of the prodigal's return. At this early point in his life, he envisioned the scene full of action, with the son's return all but crashing into his father. In contrast, the painting that Nouwen was meditating upon was from the end of Rembrandt's life, when he was broken and bereaved by life. Near death, the action had been extracted from him. Only peace and stillness remained.

The father-child relationship was not primarily about action. It was not about mission. It was certainly not about the son running away in order to get the father to notice him. The noticing was the natural state of the relationship. Rest was its language.

I had never just rested with God, my head placed against the Divine's soft belly. I had never known resting prayer; instead my prayers had always been frenetic, jumping from technique to technique, request to request. In resting prayer, I don't need an agenda. In resting prayer I can sink into sharedness.

This was when I first realized an essential idea: I am not the most important character in my spiritual story. If you were to go back through the chapters of this book, you would see that each chapter is framed around me. This is a reasonable mistake, one that I came by honestly. By and large I had been given an individualized and striving faith. That philosophy was reinforced by my perceptions, since I always appear to be the central character in every scene I have witnessed. (Think about it—is there any spiritual event my eyes have witnessed that did not rotate around me?)

But I am not the primary character; I am the responder.

How did I miss this?

Who is the subject and who is the object of Psalm 23? Who is the activating agent?

> *The Lord is my shepherd . . .*
> *He makes me lie down in green pastures;*
> *He leads me beside quiet waters.*
> *He restores my soul;*
> *He guides me in the paths of righteousness*
> *For His name's sake. . . .*
> *Your rod and Your staff, they comfort me.*
> *You prepare a table before me . . .*
> *You have anointed my head with oil.*[2]

Who is the active agent? Not me. I am not the one tasked with finding green pastures or quiet waters. I am not the one activating restoration. I am not the one guiding, comforting, preparing, or anointing. The Lord is. The Lord is.

Look at the words of the Our Father and feel the freedom of dependency:

> *Our Father who is in heaven,*
> *Hallowed be Your name.*
> *Your kingdom come.*
> *Your will be done,*
> *On earth as it is in heaven.*
> *Give us this day our daily bread.*
> *And forgive us our debts,*
> *as we also have forgiven our debtors.*
> *And do not lead us into temptation*
> *but deliver us from evil.*
> *Amen.*[3]

It was an ironically surprising gift, to be invited to rest . . . to lay my head against the Great Parent's belly and simply rest. Love wrested me from the lifestyle that had shackled me for ten years. There was nothing for me to prove, nothing for me to create, nothing for me to restore. There was certainly no hill I was responsible to conquer, battle for me to win, or mercenary endeavor for me to prove.

In the end, as the parable describes and Rembrandt's masterpiece so aptly captures, my father was not pushing me away. He was not even sending me off. There was certainly no need for me to get God to notice me. In the end, he was "watching the horizon." He was calling me to come home and rest.

NINETEEN
TEN VIRGINS

"Hallelujah!
For our Lord God Almighty reigns.
Let us rejoice and be glad
and give him glory!
For the wedding of the Lamb has come,
and his bride has made herself ready.
Fine linen, bright and clean,
was given her to wear."
—REVELATION 19:6–8[1]

SIX MONTHS. FOR SIX months I waited in Budapest. Finally the jury returned and brought the verdict.

It was concluded that I was too sick for missionary work. The solution was to send me home to Oregon and admit me to a rehab facility to detox. Initially it was a nine-month inpatient program, but the severity of my condition kept me checked in for more than three years. The facility was, in fact, a theological seminary on Portland's east side. The hope was that with a long season of treatment, I might once again become a contributing member of Christian society. Theology was my meds, lectures were my indoctrination, and research papers were my shock therapy.

I have written in other works about the challenge of those first few years back in Oregon. It was confusing and lonely. My fellow students seemed to speak a language that I couldn't understand. They had lovely little tight answers to the eternal questions posed in class. My answers came with no pretty packaging. In fact, I didn't have any answers. I had questions—raw, untamable questions—but my questions were seen as a nuisance, and more than once my professors simply shut me down. It was not their fault. They had dozens of students who "got it" and only one village idiot. I was not their constituency.

It was not all isolation and confusion. I had one friend, which is often all we need. I also had one theology professor who, at least sometimes, enjoyed my tortured bombast.

One day in class, I remember Theology Professor saying, "The most ubiquitous spiritual metaphor in the Scriptures is the marriage metaphor."

Is that true? I thought. Being the contrarian that I am, I immediately flipped through my mental files to prove him wrong. I thought of the kingdom metaphor, which appears often, especially if you consider the reigns of David and Solomon (among others) as long-form kingdom metaphor. I thought of nation metaphor, which is a huge discussion from Abraham forward, but seems to lose steam in the New Testament. The more I thought about it, the more I had to agree with Theology Professor. Marriage metaphor was certainly in the running for most ubiquitous. My internal justification went something like this:

The first marriage reference is on my Bible's second page, in Genesis 2, through the romantic companionship of Adam and Eve. The last reference is only three pages from the Bible's end in Revelation 19, with the marriage supper of the Lamb. Those are two pretty strong bookends. The in-between is pretty full as well. A huge swath of Genesis is devoted to one marriage or another: Abraham and Sarah, Isaac and Rebekah, Jacob and Leah . . . and Rachel. Ruth is a book about girl meets boy and gets married. Song of Solomon seems to be dedicated to marriage, not to mention a little "hubba-hubba." Hosea is about marriage. Jesus' first miracle is at a wedding feast in Cana. Jesus tells marriage parables: one of ten virgins waiting for a bridegroom and two about wedding banquets. Paul compares the church to a bride (in which he refers to all of us as "her." Gentlemen, congratulations, I believe we may have just been promoted).

Theology Professor, in his often-scandalous style, even used words like *conjugal* to describe our biblical relationship to God. His words were shocking, and they stuck with me. If marriage does receive that much airtime, then I have to really consider this divine marriage idea. Do I see myself as God's spouse? Should I?

These musings followed me around for months. I couldn't stop thinking about marriage. What are the active implications of this "ubiquitous metaphor"? What does this mean to my understanding of God's presence and engagement with me, and with the world?

I have to admit; this marriage idea became somehow comforting. It gave language to my often-roughshod thoughts. I liked the idea of being married to God. I liked it for a number of months.

Then something happened. It was the sort of thing that can seriously capsize your religion.

Into my life walked a woman. A real woman. Her name was Aimee. She sat just at the periphery of my existence, often at a desk in the opposite corner of my Old Testament class, just close enough that I couldn't shake her. She was almost as uncomfortable with seminary as I was. *And* she was lovely, wore glasses, had perfect cheekbones and long blond hair. She was just bohemian enough to slip through my well-formed defenses. Still, I tried to ignore her.

Exercising the willpower of Zeus, I managed to maintain my distance from her for an excruciating six months. Eventually my will was slain by a blow from my heart.

Four months of dating. Four months of engagement and *bam* . . . marriage.

I was thirty years old, and I was no longer alone. It came with all the normal perks: you don't have to drive home at the end of a long date, you get to share a sock drawer, and of course, naked wrestling. It was pretty great.

A handful of months after "I do," I was sitting at the pub, having a pint with my dear friend and theological companion, Josh. Josh has wild hair that I am convinced he keeps teased out to conceal his enormous brain. We sat together at my favorite table near the sunlight-filled front window. I had my back to the street so I could watch the wide wraparound bar for friends and other comings and goings. Josh sat across from me; our pints sat side by side on the narrow, rough-hewn table.

Josh and I were bantering about the Bible, and one of us brought up the marriage metaphor. (Josh had also enjoyed classes from Theology Professor.) Josh started out laughing about my suggestion of preaching while wearing a wedding dress. It was intended to be funny, but there was also a serious point that Josh also took to heart. With fresh inspiration, Josh started waxing about the power of that metaphor to reverse the trend of lost intimacy in our post-Enlightenment, post-Cartesian spiritualities (like I said, he is wicked smart).

While Josh was prattling on in five-syllable words, I was getting lost in my own thoughts, and as a result, was getting uncomfortable. The discomfort turned to agitation, and the agitation finally blossomed into anger. I was not angry at Josh, not at all. I was angry at the marriage metaphor.

Something had changed in me since I had first seriously pondered the marriage metaphor in that fateful theology class. My opinion of God had not changed. My desire for divine intimacy had not wavered. My affection for the institution of marriage had not waned; in fact, it had only increased. The change was this: *I was now actually married.* Marriage was no longer an abstraction; it had flesh and bone (not to mention other body parts).

The anger came on pretty strong. And the reason was clear: I had once again been sold a bill of goods. At least that is what it felt like. God had claimed in the Bible a marriage-like relationship and had not delivered . . . not even close. With Aimee, I now knew what it was to come home and have arms wrap around my neck. I knew what it was to have a lap to lay my head upon at the end of a long day. I knew what it was to lose entire evenings to lingering conversation. God was none of that. The incongruence of the marriage language was reminiscent of the triumphalistic language I had been force-fed as a child in church.

I raised my gaze up from my beer and my fretful thoughts and fired a look at Josh, who had kept talking, blissfully unaware of my internal strife. When he saw that my eyes were hot, he stopped mid-sentence and groped for his beer. He took a long draught, watching me, wide-eyed over the top of his glass. He returned the beer to the table without looking down, a remnant of foam still resting on his upper lip.

"Josh, I think we may need to reconsider our beliefs."

Josh just nodded slightly, not really sure what had just happened.

I reached into my bag and pulled out my leather-bound Bible and flopped it on the table. I frantically flipped through the front section. "I want to reexamine the marriage metaphor in the Bible. Bear with me." My mind was trying to bring some harmony back to my now angry soul (and also find language for my intuitive hunch). "Let's see, the idea of marriage is all over the Bible; that is for sure. There are married people everywhere." I kept flipping around while processing my thoughts aloud. "Adam and Eve were clearly created for each other." The pages started to turn more slowly. "But look at Isaac and Rebekah—there are two whole chapters about Isaac seeking out his bride. This is actually not about marriage; this is about their betrothal. If we look at the rest of Isaac's story, there is very little about their actual married life." I flipped a few more pages. "It is similar with Jacob and Rachel—a whole chapter about the tortured separation during betrothal and then not much about their married experience, just that they had children."

You can imagine how the rest of my diatribe went. "Look at Ruth:

almost four chapters about how she and Boaz find each other and only *three verses* about actually being married. Three!"[2]

Now I was on a roll and nothing could stop me. I went on about King Solomon and how he was clearly a marriage savant, since he had to juggle seven hundred wives. However, his actual book on romance, Song of Solomon, is much more about the pursuit of the bride than it is about union to a spouse. The romantic words are infused with the torment of their separation and the anticipation of their union at the book's end.

Hosea is as much about unrequited love as marriage itself.

Jesus did do his first miracle at a marriage feast,[3] but that is as much about the culmination of the betrothal as it is about marriage. I went on about the parables. There is one about the ten virgins.[4] It specifically tells a story of the long painful wait for the betrothed one, who has traveled a long way away. It is about engagement. The two other marriage parables are about wedding feasts,[5] but they hardly include a mention of the bride and groom. They seem more concerned about the preparation for the blessed union.

Josh was amused. The flurry of flipping pages and my frothing extemporaneous rhetoric are all things he loves about me. He was happily settling in for a conversation that he knew was just getting started.

"I am not saying that marriage is not an important metaphor in the Bible. It is. We only have to look at Ephesians 5 to see Paul's poetic writing on Christ and the church. I am absolutely not suggesting that we ignore the marriage metaphor; I just wonder if we need to elevate the betrothal metaphor. Is anybody talking about the betrothal metaphor?"

I paused for a moment to make sure that I was not journeying into heresy and total personal damnation. "I think it is telling that at the very end of the biblical story . . . the climax . . . at a time that we are called to long for, a time clearly placed in the future . . . at the Bible's culmination, there we find *our* wedding feast in Revelation 19. Right?

It appears to be the consummation of the long, long betrothal. We are literally like the ten virgins in Jesus' parable, desperately waiting for our betrothed one who has gone away on a long journey. I am not saying that we are not connected; we are. It is just not the tangible final consummation, at least not yet."

Then I had another thought: *this would harmonize with passages like . . .* I flipped back through my Bible and found these verses in Romans 8 and read to Josh: "'We ourselves, having the first fruits of the Spirit, even we ourselves groan within ourselves, waiting eagerly for *our* adoption as sons, the redemption of our body' (v. 23 NASB). In Romans, the metaphor is adoption; it is like the adoption papers have been drawn up but the actual adoption has not been totally fulfilled, and the wait leaves us groaning. Maybe our marriage papers also have been fully drawn and validated, just not yet fulfilled. Thus we groan for this as well."

I pushed the Bible away and stared at Josh.

Language is a powerful thing. Metaphor is a powerful thing.

Marriage is tangible, visceral, and conjugal, by its very nature. It is a dangerous thing to promise people a roller coaster and deliver them a little red wagon. When we use word pictures, we must consider the expectations that those pictures set up, and therefore, measure the rhetoric that we use. Metaphors can be both inspiring and destructive, at least to those of us with poets' hearts.

You may not like the betrothal metaphor. You may think that it is a gross misappropriation of Scripture. I certainly have never heard a sermon titled "You Are the Fiancé of Christ." I will, however, tell you that, while my relationship with God is precious to me, it is nothing like my relationship with my wife. The betrothal metaphor sure does line up a whole lot better with my perceivable everyday reality, much more so than does the marriage metaphor.

Theologians have terms for experiential versus linguistic discrepancies. They have had to find language for it because the discrepancy gaps are so wide. They use phrases like "now and not yet" or "positional truths." These phrases are certainly helpful to a point. But they are no longer enough for me. I must get beyond virtual beliefs.

The betrothal conversation with Josh ended up taking a number of delightful tangents about religious rhetoric and their cultural implications. In the end, Josh brilliantly connected the dots in this way: "So many religious people rail against our culture's addiction to 'virtual reality,' and yet . . ." Josh paused to measure his words, "if I am honest, it seems like many religious people, including me, are comfortable with virtual theology."

Josh and I have returned to these themes again and again over the years since. I have realized that I need categories about God that are not just true on some intangible plane. I need more than a virtual faith. I am not a video game character, and I am not an avatar. I am a person, believing alongside and integrated with other persons, and our shared personhood demands congruent relational dialogue.

For so much of my life, the religious rhetoric I had been given was wildly incongruent with my actual day-in and day-out spiritual experiences. I am not suggesting that we settle for lowballed expectations, but it is helpful to have language for the times of distance and desert, as well as language for the moments of rare intimacy and transcendence.

TWENTY
SHY

God's glory and God's shyness are one. His glory is to give
them everything and to be in the midst of them as unknown.
—*THE SIGN OF JONAS*, THOMAS MERTON

WE RELIGIOUS PEOPLE LOVE our God-talk. We are fond of using the
phrase, "God told me . . ."

"God told me to marry Jenny."

"God told me to join my church."

"God told me to sell my car."

"God told me to bet on 21-black."

Just this past week a man said to me, "God told me and my wife
to buy our new house." Just like that. His assertion was without quali-
fication. He overtly claimed divine instruction. As the conversation
went on, he admitted that the house was immense, so large that even
he could not imagine how the two of them would ever utilize even a
fraction of the size. Part of his thinking was that the house might be
used at some point as a respite for people who needed "space" (which
is something they appeared to have in grand supply).

I wonder if some of these religious phrases have become little more than socialized idioms. It is not that the words are not true, it is just that we have become so accustomed to using the phrases that we don't think about the *actual* meaning the words embody and thus neither the speaker nor the listener take them all that seriously. Here's another idiom: "That new shirt cost me *an arm and a leg*." First of all, it is hard to imagine a purchase that would justify the removal of limbs. Secondly, this term is really, really dramatic when you think about what it is saying, yet it is most often used for the purchase of something as normal as a new shirt. We all know what idioms are for. They are dramatic (unoriginal and often worn out) phrases that actually mean something far less exceptional. "That cost me an arm and a leg" really just means, "it cost me quite a bit."

I think it is the same thing with religious phrases like "God told me." We hear the pastor use such phrases all the time. "I was praying about the sermon this past week, and God told me to speak about . . ." When the pastor uses this phrase, I don't believe that she or he actually heard God's audible voice. I don't believe that a burning bush appeared on her desk or a dove descended inside his church office. When the pastor says something like "God told me," I actually believe that they meant, "I had an inclination as to what I wanted to speak about this week, and my strong suspicion was that God would approve of the topic." However, it is just easier and more commonplace to say, "God told me."

Let's take the example of the man I spoke to this last week. Did he really mean that God spoke to him about a certain house? Did he really hear God "tell" him to buy it? Did the house smell of tabernacle incense or come with the manifestations of Moses and Elijah? I sincerely doubt it. When he said, "God told us," I believe this man was saying, "We found a house we love (maybe it even reminds us of God's abundant love for us), and it is a place that we suspect God will use in us and around us."

The funny thing is that when I hear people tell stories of when God does actually speak to them, they don't tend to bluntly say, "God told me." Instead there is most often a far more elaborate story, full of more carefully constructed and original language and metaphor. We only use idioms for common talk. It is often the product of lazy communication.

Language is important, and it often sets up odd and secret expectations within us. When we throw around phrases like "God spoke to me," it can seed doubt in the heart when someone is not feeling "God speaking." It places a subversive need in some to pretend their faith is more than it actually is (and so they adopt the exaggerated language to support their pretending). These exaggerations tend to create profound incongruence between the believing person's dialogue and their actual life with God. Their words (internal and external) paint God as chatty, when in fact, God is most often shy.

———

I have been taught about the Holy Spirit all my life. The Holy Spirit is the one who fills us. Some believe that the Holy Spirit provides an additional baptism into a more supercharged spiritual life. The Holy Spirit is a provider of truth, a guide, and the convicter of righteousness. Whatever the specifics, Jesus once wrote that he would send the Spirit as the one who will walk by our side. The word is sometimes translated, "Helper."

Not long ago, I heard the Holy Spirit referred to as "shy." That was an odd thing to say about the Divine Spirit. However, the more I thought about it, the more I understood this unusual identification.

Isn't it interesting that the copowerful, coeternal, co-Creator with the Father and the Son would get so little airtime? As I flip through the pages of my Bible, the Holy Spirit seems to consistently take a backseat to the two more famous Trinitians. When the Holy Spirit does appear or is mentioned as an active character in a scene, does the Spirit ever speak? I am sitting here trying to think of a time when actual words are attributed to the Holy Spirit's voice. I am sure there are some, but none immediately come to mind. I am sure the Spirit is able to speak, however the actual words are few, shockingly few.

This silent Divine is the member of the triune godhead that has been tasked with caring for us. Jesus said, "It is to your advantage that I go away; for if I do not go away, the Helper will not come to you; but if I go, I will send Him to you ... when He, the Spirit of truth, comes, He will guide you into all truth."[1]

This is our companion? This is the one that we are called to rely upon? This is the one who walks by our side ... *the one who hardly speaks?*

If the Spirit is quiet and shy through the pages of my Bible, then why would I expect this introvert to suddenly start rambling on to me like a tipsy busybody?

Maybe this is the very heart of my problem. Have I falsely married God's tangibility with God's presence? Have I falsely conflated "God speaking" with God's companionship?

The Holy Spirit may be the Bible's perfect example of a faithful but silent escort. What would it look like to rest in the Spirit's ever-presence as such? What if I expressed my gratitude for the Spirit's companionship even without tangible evidence? That kind of sounds like faith, doesn't it?

On the other hand, faith is really hard. It is hard to live in the silence. It is hard to accept the shyness. And, more often than not, I want what I want, when I want it.

TWENTY-ONE
BUFFET FAITH

*Lord, my face reddens with shame realizing that I go to your altar
and the table of holy communion with a tepid and indifferent heart.*
—THOMAS À KEMPIS

PEOPLE ARE AFRAID OF hell.

I wonder if people are afraid of hell, not because they are afraid
of God's judgment, but because *they are afraid that God will give them
what they want.*

The process of understanding my deeper desires (my wants) is
a challenging process. It requires unraveling layers of selfish techniques and validation systems.

I have many friends who are older-than-average bachelors. They
have made it to their thirties or even forties still single. These men
are often talented, intelligent, decent looking, and even reasonably
successful in either the corporate or church world. They inevitably
lament to me about their inability to find a mate. I try to be patient
with them. I try to be a good friend who listens to their plight and the
correlated "pain" that they feel. They graphically explain to me about

their loneliness and their sadness of undiscovered companionship. However, when I truly press them about their deeper longings, asking them about the girls who have come and gone and the innumerable opportunities missed, the answer is usually some combination of: 1) The process of getting married (dating, engagement, wedding, marriage transition) would derail other goals, and 2) What if someone better comes along?

In the end, the preference for convenience and staying available for better opportunities were the stronger desires, stronger than the longing for companionship. Ultimately it is not about one's romantic desires. It is about their deeper wants.

Do I really want God? I believe I do.

Do I want to be with God? This is certainly *one* of my many desires.

Back to the question of hell. Regardless of whether you believe it to be metaphoric or actual, symbolic or tangible, there is very little we actually know about the place "down there." One thing we do know is that in the concept of hell, God is at a relational distance. Functionally, God is not present. It is not God's realm. So the question of hell and my wants could be as simple as, "Do I actually want God?" If I truly want God, in my deeper spaces, then I want heaven. If I don't want God, then . . . let's just say that hell might have a door that opens from the outside.

Does that make sense?

It begs to reason then, that if I do want God with me, I may need to accept God's full package. Like the bachelor's quandry above, I need to ask myself, "Is God important enough to me to accept the inconvenience and potential sacrifice of my other priorities? Accepting God is certainly about experiencing God's love, receiving eternal fulfillment, experiencing forgiveness, receiving a spiritual family, and stepping into the manifestation of my created purpose. However, it might mean a whole lot more than that. That is, for instance, if I take Jesus at his word.

It would, therefore, mean that I would have to figure out how to "love my enemy and pray for those who persecute." It would mean that I would have to "turn the other cheek" and "rejoice in pain." It would certainly mean that I would have to give up my coat to anyone who asks (and apparently my cloak as well), and it would require a constant willingness to drop whatever I was doing to walk "the extra mile" with anyone who asked. It would mean not worshipping until I have forgiven everyone whom I have cause against and begging for forgiveness from anyone who has cause against me. It would mean feeding those who are hungry, clothing those who are naked, visiting those in prison, caring for those who are sick, and inviting in the stranger. It might also mean that I need to sell all I have and give to the poor. And it might mean that I have to learn how to pray that mountains might be cast into the sea.

Do I really want that kind of God? I know that I would prefer a buffet-line God, the sort where I get to pick and choose what I want from the divine agenda. God can have my Sunday morning and my Wednesday evening and one week each summer, but I get the rest. God can have my 10 percent, but he does not get access to my retirement funds (even though Jesus spoke out against the man who stored up enough wealth for years). I am willing to submit to the "church" as long as I get to pick and choose which branches (or twigs) of the church I submit to, and as long as the authorities in those branches have the same value system as me, *and* as long as I reserve the right to cut and run anytime the church no longer meets my needs. Certainly don't ask me to submit to those parts of the church that are very different than I am.

In my petulance, I often want to point at God and complain. "Why don't you show up more? Why don't you show up in my pain? Why don't you speak to me like you speak to others?" And yet, if I am honest, I am unwilling to process the question, "Do I even want God?" Seriously. Do I want the Jesus-Way? Or do I actually want a religious system of my own creation, like my plate at the end of a buffet counter, filled with only my favorite and tasty items? And if I only want a buffet-religion of my own creation, then it would make sense that prayer feels an awful lot like talking to myself.

If I don't really want God, then maybe God is just being hospitable. God is simply giving me what I want.

TWENTY-TWO
GOD IS BLACK

Red and yellow, black and white,
They are precious in his sight.
—A SUNDAY SCHOOL SONG

ABOUT FIVE YEARS AGO, I was sitting in "group." I had been attending this three-hour (and then some) weekly gathering for more than three years. I felt like I should have been given a coin to commemorate the anniversary. "Hello, my name is Tony (Hello, Tony), and this is my one hundred and fiftieth meeting."

This circle had in many ways become my church. It was a gathering of haggard and often caustic Jesus-followers. The circle was made up of around twenty-five men. Half the circle was white. If you only counted the white guys, it would still have been the most diverse circle I had ever sat in: millionaires and dudes on welfare, lawyers and ex-cons, sixty-year-olds and twenty-year-olds, lifelong church addicts and brand new converts.

But the circle wasn't just white. In fact it was arguably the most racially diverse circle in all of Portland. There were about a dozen black guys: Uncle Larry, Jeff, Greg, "Pops," Steve, John, Freddie, and so on. There were a couple of scholarly Native Americans, and there was a defensive-lineman-sized Mexican kid named Ovi.

The significance of this diverse reality would be clearer if you knew more about Portland. While being a city with a great reputation of enlightenment, tolerance, and acceptance, Portland has a barbaric racial record. Up until the year 2000, the state constitution still contained language like: "No Negro . . . shall come, reside, or be within this State, or hold any real estate." As late as the year 2002, a professor of Portland history told me that 90 percent of all African Americans in the entire state of Oregon lived within three-quarters of a mile of the intersection of Killingsworth and Albina in north Portland (an intersection less than half a mile from my house). There is a word for that: *segregation*. Only an hour ago, I was on the phone with a buddy of mine who lives in bohemian and artistic southeast Portland, and unprompted, he made this statement: "I live in the whitest neighborhood in America. I see a black person maybe once a year." That is clearly an exaggeration, but you get the idea. In Portland, at least historically, the races don't mix.

And yet there I was, staring around the circle. I was still a rookie to these ranks, even after three faithful years. Some of these guys had been meeting together for two decades. They were the elders of the group. These men were becoming my uncles and my brothers. The truth was we hated and loved each other, depending upon the week, but we were committed to stay together and discover together the way of Jesus, across racial lines, all bathed in the fire of honest prejudice and reconciliation. You couldn't even say that we were unified around "faith," even though we were all Jesus-people, because there were so many different perspectives on what "faith" means. Instead, we were unified by a person: Jesus.

How did I get here? Well, that is a long story. I will try to be brief. The beginning may surprise you.

About five years before this, I was sitting in a theological lecture in a dank basement classroom. The topic was the Trinity. It was more than just a discussion of God's triune nature; it was an overview of trinitarianism, a term that was new to me. As a lifelong Christian churchgoer, I had seemingly always known about the Trinity, but that day's perspective was different. The redheaded speaker posted a sixteenth-century Russian icon on the screen behind him. Growing up, I had been taught to be critical of icons, but this one cut past my programming. Beauty can do that.

The icon depicted three figures sitting around a table together. They were obviously heavenly beings, with faces alight and winged bodies. The man explained that it is essential to understand that an icon like this one, "The Icon of the Holy Trinity," is not a picture of God. It is, instead, a representation of a theology about God. An icon is a theological writing from an ancient time, a time when visual metaphors were more accessible than literate words.

The icon represented three heavenly figures lost in love with one another. It was a metaphor of swirling affection, of eternal communion, and of God's sacrificial nature.

I remember him saying something like, "One of the mistakes of Christianity is that we tend to think of God as either One Being, as the Shema rightly tells us—'Hear O Israel, the LORD our God, the LORD is one'—or as three persons: Father, Son, and Holy Spirit. What we miss is that God is also essentially Community. God is not only one-in-three and three-in-one. God is also the plural singularity. God is communal."

Often, personal transformation does not come from new information; it comes from new emphasis. This redheaded theologian was emphasizing an aspect of God in a way that I had not considered before. What if God was, in fact, primarily communal? How would that affect the way that I believe? How would that affect the way that I live?

The first impact was a simple one. It brought to bear a foundational trinitarian passage from Genesis 1:

Let Us create humankind in Our image . . .
Let Us create them male and female.[1]

Here God seems to agree with the redheaded theologian. God refers to Godself as "Us" and "Our." God's self-declared identity is communal.

Then, and this is where the concept really jumps my Western-trained mental rails, God confers on humanity that same identity construct. Based on the statement in Genesis, we must consider that our identity is communal as well.

This revelation brought so many of my experiences overseas to bear. Albanians, for example, are a very ancient people. When I arrived, their culture had been fairly untainted by Western society, with its emphasis on the individual. Albanians tended to refer to themselves in communal terms, not individual terms. They appealed to their identity as a part of a larger communal reality: family, tribe, nation, village. As a young man, this orientation created dissonance in me, because I had been programmed to be an individual. This individualism (addiction) came from my culture, my education, my religion, and most specifically, my pioneer family roots.

Around this same time, I also started thinking about my Bible differently. It never occurred to me how much I read God's Word in individualistic terms, as if it was a document written directly to me, my own personal religious document. My schooling, at the time, required me to acquire a rudimentary understanding of the original language of my New Testament. I did not have the ability to make nuanced and profound interpretations, but there were some blatantly obvious ones that hit me in the face. From the Greek language, I learned that the majority of the spiritual identity statements of Scripture were not about individuals. The terms were communal (excuse the Southern colloquialism—there is just not another good word in English): "Y'all shall be to me sons and daughters" (2 Cor. 6:18, paraphrase). "Y'all received a spirit of adoption" (Rom. 8:15, paraphrase). "Faithful is the One who calls y'all" (1 Thess. 5:24, paraphrase). "Y'all are being justified by a gift of his grace" (Rom. 3:24, paraphrase). "Y'all who were far away are being brought near by Christ's blood" (Eph. 2:13, paraphrase). The list goes on and on.

I know, I know, this is all pretty Sunday school stuff, but it was bending my view of reality. Up to this point, I had mostly only conceived of God as an individual. I had only conceived of myself as an individual, but now . . .

Maybe in my individualistic addiction I had missed the fact that God wanted to encounter me as a communal being. Maybe one of the reasons my spiritual ears had problems "hearing" God was because they had been tuned to only individualistic frequencies.

Aimee and I started to rethink the structure of our lives. This concept led us to try to integrate ourselves with others. We opened our home. We lived communally with others. We tried to exist in active submission among communities. It was all baby steps . . . nothing impressive, but to us, it felt like faith leaps.

We didn't stop there. There was another angle of this communal theology that we struggled to integrate. The Trinity was also the essence of diversity: eternally diverse creativity, eternally diverse gifting, eternally diverse expressivity, eternally diverse personality, and so on. God is "unity *in* diversity": the essence of unity and the essence of diversity. All hope for unity emanates from God. All hope for diversity emanates from God. And we have been made together in God's image.

My theology of God had been so small, so simplistic that I had not even realized that God is the most diverse communal being imaginable, beyond imagination in fact. This diversity is wider than the universe and more complex than cosmic history. And thus, God is ever inviting us more and more deeply into unified diversity.

I was coming to see that God's unyielding commitment to this unity in diversity was (at least part of) why the Holy Spirit baptized the story of the church with a shockingly diverse miracle:

> All of them were filled with the Holy Spirit and began to speak in other tongues as the Spirit enabled them. . . . Parthians, Medes and Elamites; residents of Mesopotamia, Judea and Cappadocia, Pontus and Asia, Phrygia and Pamphylia, Egypt and the parts of Libya near Cyrene; visitors from Rome (both Jews and converts to Judiasm); Cretans and Arabs. (Acts 2:4, 9–11 NIV)

And it is also why the climax of this human spiritual story is expressed in a heavenly vision that is the epitome of human diversity:

> After these things I looked, and behold, a great multitude which no one could count, *from every nation and all tribes and peoples and tongues*, standing before the throne and before the Lamb. (Revelation 7:9 NASB, emphasis mine)

God's commitment to "unity in diversity" was written plainly in the pages of my Bible. The challenge for my young family was that even though our home was "open" and our lifestyle was "communal," the natural traffic of society seemed to only draw us to people who were more or less just like us. It brought people who were lovely and prioritized the spiritual, but by and large everyone was white. They were middle class. They were around our age. They were university educated. We tended to read the same books, join the same organizations, vote along similar lines, and enjoy the same recreations. Our life was far from the picture of God's people of Acts 2 or the prophetic image of Revelation 7.

We felt paralyzed to imagine our life any other way. It was the only programming we knew.

One morning, I had breakfast with Kurt. We were just becoming friends. He was a successful businessman, and I had a failing business. He was theologically astute and had lived more life than I had, and he had graciously agreed to an early meeting.

It was an enjoyable discussion. I appreciated Kurt's ideas, and he was more than once surprised by mine. At the end of our breakfast, Kurt looked at me with a quizzical gleam in his eye. He was stuck midthought, as if he was weighing whether he wanted to make his offer.

After a short pause, he chose to take the risk. "I want you to come to my group. I will be there at seven in the morning . . . if you are willing, meet me there." And with that, our breakfast was done.

A couple of days later, there I was, sitting in the circle, surrounded by these Sons of Thunder, men of power and intuition who came together every week to wrestle through the stuff of faith, God, and humanity.

There is magic in a circle like this one. It is not hocus-pocus; it is a magical shattering of unspoken societal patterns. The vast majority of societal patterns gather people into affinity organizations. What I mean is, there are forces all around us (and within us) that cause us to want to be with people who are just like we are. Rich people tend to gather with rich people and poor with poor. We stick to our cultural subgroups. We tend to organize in racial and class distinctions. We are naturally drawn according to political, educational, and recreational distinctions. You could say that this is most evidenced in the Christian church of North America. Dr. Martin Luther King Jr. said, "Eleven o'clock on a Sunday morning is one of the most, if not *the* most, segregated hour in Christian America."

In our affinity gatherings we make unspoken contracts with one another. There are ideas that we are allowed to explore (and others that we are not), sins we are willing to confront (and others that we silently agree to ignore), and we subtly enable together our shared lifestyle patterns. All of this is quite easy since we all come from a similar background; we tend to have all the same blind spots. With no "minority report" present to change the rhythm of exchange, the group tends to continue on the same, year after year. It is no wonder that so many churches feel like they never "grow deeper" or expand to new forms of transformation.

My new "group" intentionally existed to shatter those patterns. Young people were invited to confront the elders in the group. Poor men could prophetically speak into the lives of the rich. And, Lord have mercy, the African Americans took our white behinds to task.

There are many times that I have found myself on the operating table of this communal confrontation. My prejudices, my patterns of false validation, my arrogance, my cowardice—these were all the open privy of the circle. It was a process that we referred to as "surgery without anesthesia," and while on one hand I wouldn't recommend it, there may, in fact, be no greater gift.

My Uncle Richard, who died unexpectedly this year, is a Lakota Sioux, born on the Rosebud Reservation of South Dakota. He was a husband, a father, a friend, a scholar, and a dear resident of our circle. Uncle Richard once said, "Before I entered the circle, I never knew that God was black. I had never before heard God speak to me through the mouth of a black man." And when I look around our circle, I am learning to understand exactly what he means.

There is a unique power when we dare to listen to God speak to us through the mouth of those who are radically other, to discover that God is black, God is red, God is poor, incarcerated, sick, or a stranger ("as much as you have done it to the least of these, you have done it unto me").

This life with the other is about more than the occasional conversation; I believe it must exist in a profound life of being. The men of the circle, they see me most every day. They know, not just my problems and my pathologies, but my wife. They are helping me raise my sons. They are curating my dreams. And slowly I am learning to more fully submit, trusting that they are an essential element of God's voice to me.

It is little more than experiencing our identity as God intended. For as God has always been, so we long to be: unity in diversity.

Just as a body, though one, has many parts, but all its many parts form one body, so it is with Christ. For we were all baptized by one Spirit so as to form one body—whether Jews or Gentiles, slave or free—and we were all given the one Spirit to drink. Even so the body is not made up of one part but of many. . . . The eye cannot say to the hand, "I don't need you!" And the head cannot say to the feet, "I don't need you!" . . . If one part suffers, every part suffers with it; if one part is honored, every part rejoices with it. Now you are the body of Christ, and each one of you is a part of it. (1 Corinthians 12:12–14, 21, 26–27 NIV)

TWENTY-THREE
THAT WHICH IS COMMON

"Blessed are the poor ..."
—MATTHEW 5:3[1]

THERE HAVE BEEN MORE than a few times that my wife, Aimee, and I have descended to the bottom of our financial reserves. We have not been the types to waste money (at least by Western standards); I just have not been very good at making it. There have been several times when we were ten days short of the month's end and out of funds, only to find an anonymous envelope on the front step with a few hundred dollars, usually just enough to get us through. We never advertised that it was a "bad month," but the money showed up anyway. Do you think God had something to do with that?

I can remember one time, our fridge was pretty darn empty. I remember the amount in the bank: twenty dollars. Despite that reality, life goes on. Unexpectedly, my buddy Bryan invited us to watch him perform at the Highland Games, sponsored by MacTarnahan's beer. He was competing in the caber toss. (A caber is essentially a telephone pole that you pick up and attempt to throw for distance; you can easily imagine why Bryan wanted an audience.) We told him that we were broke, but he insisted that the entrance fee was only a couple dollars and he *reeeeallly* wanted us to come. So we figured, *what the heck*. If you are gonna spend your last few dollars, might as well do it in style. We loaded our infant son and black-and-grey mastiff into our rusted-out silver Volvo station wagon and hoped there was enough gas to get us to the gaming grounds and back.

We made it, only to learn that the entrance fee was eight dollars a person. Our hearts sank. That amount we simply could not justify. It was a hard decision to leave, but what could we do? It felt like a wasted trip. Maybe we could find a nice spot on the way home to walk Simon. (Simon is the name of the dog, not the infant.) We made the difficult choice, and I ran off to find a way to sneak into the grounds and tell Bryan, "We can't afford to stay."

While I was gone, Aimee sat down under a tree, not far from the stadium's main entrance. I caught a back entrance door as it was closing, slipped in, and after about fifteen minutes, found Bryan. He was disappointed we couldn't stay, but of course understood.

I returned to my family after maybe a half-hour gone to find them engaged with an elderly man who had fallen in love with our brindled mastiff. The man was chatty, and Aimee seemed happy to let the old fellow coo and nuzzle our dog.

A few minutes later, a driver rode up in a golf cart and the elderly man climbed in. Before it pulled away, he turned to me and asked how we were enjoying the games. I gave him an embarrassed smile and explained to him that we had not realized the price of entrance. It was more than we could afford, so we were regrettably headed back home.

At this, the codger tipped his head back and roared with laughter. Then he declared, like a character in a children's Christmas claymation special, "No one comes to my games and doesn't enjoy at least one pint of my beer." (Okay, maybe not a children's special, but you get the idea.) We followed him as he drove unquestioned through the front gates and down to the VIP tent at the games' center.

The rest of the day we ate and drank on the tab of Ole Mac

MacTarnahan, the founder of MacTarnahan's beer. We got to watch Bryan toss the caber. Our bank account and our gas tank were running on fumes, yet for one spring afternoon, we lived like kings and hadn't a worry in the world.

Now, what are the odds? What are the chances that we would foolishly attempt to watch our friend when we couldn't shop for food, and then what are the chances that Ole Mac would meet us, adopt us, and treat us to opulence? What role does your understanding of God play in a scenario like this one? Any?

This story is dangerously close to the slot-machine concept of God, isn't it? *Just pull the handle and see what happens.*

Whatever this story says about God, there was something more foundational that I believe God wanted to teach us in this delicate season.

Our on-again, off-again financial struggles were a minor problem when we considered the global picture. It was the stuff of entitlement, the sorts of financial problems that "oppress" twenty-first-century westerners. We had never watched our babies go hungry. We had never been turned out on the street. We had never been marginalized by society because of our economic "status" or caste. But just because we lived in the luxury of Western society, that doesn't mean that God did not have things to show us.

Around this same time, the time of the Highland Games, my household (my family and our housemates) was hosting a small faith-community. We met on Tuesday evenings and were trying to practice the Jesus-Way together. It was pretty normal stuff: Bible reading, prayer, and the occasional act of service.

On this occasion, one of our members had set up an appointment for all of us to visit the Oregon Food Bank. The main bank warehouse for the entire state was less than a mile from our home, and it seemed like a great way to volunteer.

About twenty of us met at the bank and, for a few hours, helped sort food and bag vegetables. We laughed and told stories around the giant bins filled with locally grown green beans.

Afterward, we were offered a tour of the warehouse. A food bank staff member led us around, and let me assure you, I was not prepared for what I saw.

We followed her into a space larger than an airplane hangar; the scaffolding of stacked food pallets rose several stories into the air. As we walked through the crate-built chasms, forklifts on steroids scurried up and down the box canyons like giant droids.

Our guide was casual, comfortable with her well-rehearsed script. She walked backward in front of us, playing the role of our eyes, since we were all lost in the food reserves that climbed to the ceiling. She rattled off numbers that were surely impressive, though mostly impractically large: x number of tons of food shipped each day, x number of vegetables augmenting x amount of nutrition each month . . .

Then, before one busy intersection, she stopped. She raised her hands both to get us to stop and to grab our attention. "Each year at least one in ten Oregonian families will require at least one emergency food box. A food box contains a two-week supply of nutrition for a family of four. Yes, you heard me correctly: one in ten."

The number was shocking to me. *How was that possible? How could there be so many poor people in my state? We must do something about it. We must double our efforts to support all those poor families out there.*

My thoughts were as compassionate as they were condescending. That's right, condescending.

In the midst of my blind condescension, I had the following sensation. Standing there between a three-story tower of canned meats and stacked beans, I had the clear feeling of being swatted across the back of the head. No one had touched me; the swat came from no human. The corresponding thought that ran into my brain was this: *You, fool. It's you! She is talking about you. You are poor. You need help. You are the one in ten. You are the needy she is talking about.*

This is not a story about government programs. It is not even a story about caring for the poor or the social responsibilities of God's people. It is a story about classism. That's right, classism; particularly the classism that exists inside of me. The insidious ways that I believe I am different (better) than other people on an identity level. I am talking about those corrupt beliefs that keep me locked away from large swaths of my fellow humans (and from reality as God intended).

It did not matter that my refrigerator was empty. It didn't matter that we had no money in the bank. I didn't matter that we couldn't pay our bills. We were simply *not* poor.

As the rest of our group began again to follow our host between the stacks, I stayed back alone, oblivious to the crowd of shoulders bumping past me. I repented of my narrow-mindedness and my judgment. "Poor" to me was not an economic condition; it was a statement of identity: people in ghettos are poor, Albanians are poor, and people who take public assistance are poor. I could never be poor.

With resignation and an odd sensation of gratitude, I began at that moment to say to myself, slowly at first: *We are poor . . . We are poor . . . We are poor.*

Our shared humanity is about more than our words. A true egalitarianism requires a transformation of our hearts, where we actually believe that we are all equal.

No temptation has overtaken you except what is common to humankind. (1 Cor. 10:13 NIV, paraphrase)

There is neither Jew nor Greek, there is neither slave nor free man, there is neither male nor female; for you all are one in Christ Jesus. (Gal. 3:28 NASB)

Give us this day, our daily bread. (Matt. 6:11 NASB, emphasis added)

> *Blessed are the poor in spirit . . . those who mourn . . . the*
> *gentle . . . those who hunger and thirst for righteousness . . .*
> *the merciful . . . the pure in heart . . . the peacemakers . . .*
> *those who have been persecuted.* (Matt. 5:3–10 NASB)

> *"Let Us create humankind in Our image . . ."*
> (Gen. 1:26 NIV, paraphrase)

I wonder . . . I just wonder how many of the short circuits in my communication lines with God exist because of my small-mindedness toward my fellow humans. There are seemingly endless ways that I define myself as "better than" (and also "worse than") and therefore separate myself from humanity's shared life, as God did not intend. I use hierarchical categories of economics, class, race, culture, gender, politics, and preferences to elevate myself above my human sister or brother. In the above story, I was sympathetic about the poor; you could even say that I "loved" them. But I was unable to see myself as one with them. They were relegated to a different, and regrettably condescended, category.

What if I really believed in an integrated identity with all people? What if I believed in a shared life and a shared spirituality? What if we even had a shared communication with God?

Back decades ago, before cell phones, even before landlines were considered common, if you wanted to have a phone in your home, you had to have a party line. A party line meant that if you wanted to communicate by phone, you had to be willing to share the line with your "neighbors." Maybe transcendent communication also requires a party line with humanity. The more we are truly *with* the other (if not literally, then at least free of hierarchical judgment in our hearts), maybe we will find our hearts more aligned with the Divine, through God's created intent.

My friend Ken Loyd says that the Lord's Prayer, the prayer Jesus taught us to pray in Matthew 6, will never make sense until we figure out who the "us" is. The phrase "Give us this day our daily bread" makes no sense until we embody the reality that we are begging God within our shared and communal identity as cohumanity.

And maybe, just maybe, I will discover that God is not speaking to *me* because God is waiting to speak to *us*.

TWENTY-FOUR
REPELLED

God made him who had no sin to be sin for us, so that
in him we might become the righteousness of God.
—2 CORINTHIANS 5:21[1]

THE THEOLOGY I HAVE been given throughout my life is clear. Jesus had to die on a cross in order to erase my sin. Why did Jesus have to erase my sin? Because God cannot stand to be in the presence of sin. If there is any hope for me to be with God, my sin must be gone.

As a young man, this theology gave me hope. Not just because I had received the gift of forgiveness, kneeling on the floor of my grandmother's family room. It also gave me hope because, by and large, I believed I had kicked the habitual presence of sin. More often than not, I believed I was a venerable example of Christian morality and, based on the Top 40 list of sins, I was doing quite well. I had managed to keep my private parts to myself. I rarely drank, had never smoked, didn't gamble, didn't swear. Like I said, pretty impressive. Outside of the occasional crippling seasons of doubt, I was on pretty solid ground.

I became so impressed with my own press that I actually had the following experience. I was walking alone, in the sun, down Monroe

Avenue in Corvallis, Oregon. It was during my furlough in my mid-twenties. It was only a few months before my cabin getaway in the Cascade mountains, when I believed God confirmed my "call" to move to Macedonia. I strolled along toward American Dream Pizza. My mind was free floating. I had no particular agenda. Then this thought slipped into my consciousness. I don't know where it came from. It just floated in and landed on my mind like a butterfly: *I wonder if I am even a sinner?*

At the time, this horrifying thought hardly fazed me. It seemed like a reasonable assessment of my spiritual circumstance. A handful of years later, after my failure in Macedonia and the confrontation with my shame, I understood that my religiousness had masked a lifelong insidiousness. My presumed "righteousness" may have been my greatest sin of all.

What am I to do with a God who is repelled by sin? I am a sinner. It is undeniable. I suspect that I am even a particularly barbaric sinner. If God is repelled by sin, then it is only logical that *God is repelled by me.*

A few years ago, I was sitting at a boardroom table in an inner-Portland coffee shop. Around the table sat a traveling ministry team from Brownwood, Texas. They had come to Portland to witness ministry perspectives in a post-Christian city. I think they believed Portland provided as great a contrast to their native Texas as India or Egypt would.

On this afternoon, I had invited crazy-haired Josh to come and share some of his thoughts on life and ministry. Josh never fails to provide students with a thought-provoking discussion.

I don't remember all that Josh said, but I do remember this. He was expressing a critique of many Christians' perspective on the message of Jesus. He was sharing about the wonder of God, the constant presence of God, and the work of redemption that God is ever-performing in the world. At one poignant moment in his presentation, Josh stopped and with one hand extended, palm up, he looked around the table at each set of eyes. "The reality of the gospel is this." He paused again. "God is not repelled by our sin. Our sin is repelled by God."

There it is.

I cannot speak for the rest of the table, but I was stunned by the simplicity and clarity of his statement. Josh went on to say, "God is unhindered. We want to say that it is God's power that leaves God unhindered, but it is not God's love of power; it is God's power to love. God loves you. There is nothing that you could do that would keep God from you. We too often get it backward. We do not experience God by avoiding sin, we overcome sin by pressing into God." Josh went on to describe how this theme saturates the narrative of Scripture: Adam and Eve sinned and hid, but God chased them in the garden. Moses came down the mountaintop bearing how God wanted to be known, but the people ran away and covered Moses's face. Jesus, ultimately, came down the mountain like Moses, bearing the glory of God, and we pushed him away and killed him. God is coming after us and is *not* repelled by our sin. What would it look like to stop running and receive God's pursuit?

Josh's words were a melody to my soul. I found myself thinking about it time and again in the weeks that followed. I was not sure how to apply the ideas, but they stayed with me all the same. I had assumed that God kept distant from me because of my sin saturation. Is it possible that I had missed something profound and primal?

Then time passed. Eventually life took over, and like so many lessons, Josh's words leaked out of my regular thoughts. I went about life, distracted as always by the tyranny of the urgent.

Then one day, a bad day, I entered once again into my sinsanity. On this day, I slid inexcusably into sin—slimy, self-serving sin. Like so many sin episodes, it came upon me unexpectedly and soon took me over.

In that very moment, a single thought assaulted my chaos. The thought was this: *God is not repelled by my sin. My sin is repelled by God.*

Then and there, sin still in hand and soiled by my shame, the sense of God's presence came upon me. It would do me no service to cheapen the moment with religious words. God simply was.

It was nothing more than participating in the gospel narratives. Jesus was not repelled by sin. He was comfortable with a presumed prostitute running her fingers through his hair or massaging his feet with oil. He was enthusiastic, even insistent to enter the house of a "sinner." And what happened when he entered? Systemic and habitual sin was confessed, and restitution was made. Like a holiness typhoon, sin was blown from the room.

In the end, it says, "He who knew no sin, became sin on our behalf, so we might become the righteousness of God."[2] Now I ask you, was Jesus repelled by sin, or was sin repelled by Jesus?

Maybe God is not present with me more often because I have belittled God's love, relegated his interest in me only to my "righteous" behaviors, and denied his invading companionship in the very moments I most need his repelling presence.

God is not repelled by my sin. My sin is repelled by God.

TWENTY-FIVE
THE ONE BEHIND EVERYTHING

God
And I have become
Like two giant fat people
Living in a
Tiny boat.
We
Keep
Bumping into each other and
L
a
u
g
h
i
n
g
.

—"TWO GIANT FAT PEOPLE," *THE GIFT*, HAFIZ

THIS PAST SUMMER I was driving up over the Mount Hood pass into central Oregon. I was inside my rattletrap Volvo, climbing the cliff-top winding highway toward the pass's summit. I had no intention of encountering God, but in a rare moment, it felt like God encountered me.

The divine presence came to me in the waves of beauty washing over me through the grandeur of creation. The mythical Northwest forests wrap around those Cascade peaks. With each new bend in the road, another wave of green breaks over the one before. Rise and crash, rise and crash, rise and crash, like the sea swells against the Pacific coast. There is one long turn along the narrow highway, where as you surface through the arching bend, the wall of trees climbs and climbs above you like a cresting tsunami, the cascade of green so tall it slices the roof of blue in half.

I have driven this road dozens and dozens of times before, but I had never recognized its true majesty as I did that day. Never before had the presence of God so bellowed at me through that great swath of creation.

At this very moment of Creator-communication, as the waves of green crashed over my car, the following words burst through my mind:

Be praised for all Your tenderness by these works of Your hands
Suns that rise and rains that fall to bless
and bring to life Your land
Look down upon this winter wheat and
be glad that You have made
Blue for the sky and the color green that
fills these fields with praise

This instant of inspiration and tenderness lit the tinder in my brain. The world slowed down and my thoughts soared forward. My soul felt inexplicably tuned to a heavenly signal. My mind was processing at a daunting speed, as if God's finger was reaching down and stirring the inside of my skull, stimulating my breakneck musings: thoughts of my family, dreams for my boys, perspectives on my purpose, peace over opportunities lost, hope for the future, critiques of my false validations. My thoughts were splashing over the top of one another inside me even more quickly than the waves of forest green all around me.

It was the most unexpected mystical moment, unlike anything I had felt in a long, long time . . . maybe even since the fateful day with Jesus in my Macedonian bedroom almost fifteen years before. I had no explanation for why God would want to lift me up so high, high in the air.

I would, however, not have to wait long to learn at least a portion of the reason why.

Time passed. Maybe thirty minutes later, I was rolling down the backside of Mount Hood. As I descended, my mind, which had been racing so quickly, slowly downshifted. The highway flattened out into the Warm Springs Reservation, and the rez dumps into my father's childhood ranch-town. There in the high desert of central Oregon, my dammed-up sorrow broke out within me. The loved ones I had lost that last year rushed upon me: the death of my dad, the death of my grandmother soon after him, the death of my dear mentor and friend Richard Twiss, and of course the suffering of my sweet nephew, Ransom. The mile markers passed by me like blows from a boxing glove, releasing my mourning from deep within. The groaning was fierce and, to be honest, long overdue.

God had lifted me up so high on that mountain pass, I believe, because God knew how far I was about to freefall. I needed to soar and so, for those few precious moments, God had mercifully tuned my soul to heaven.

I wish you could have met my Uncle Richard, weathered by life and filled with wisdom. He lived his life as a profound follower of the

Jesus-Way. Before he died, he told me that his favorite quote about God was by a Persian poet named Hafiz. The poem goes like this:

> *God*
> *And I have become*
> *Like two giant fat people*
> *Living in a*
> *Tiny boat.*
> *We*
> *Keep*
> *Bumping into each other and*
> *L*
> *a*
> *u*
> *g*
> *h*
> *i*
> *n*
> *g*
> *.*

Uncle Richard managed to live his life with a very different understanding of God's nearness than mine. Maybe his many decades had allowed his soul to find God's frequency in a way that mine hadn't. Maybe his many pains and trials had smudged the cynicism from his heart. Maybe it was his indigenous roots that simply gave his spirit perspectives on God that my Anglo-addictions crippled me from experiencing. Whatever it is, I long to encounter God as he and Hafiz envisioned.

One of Uncle Richard's best friends and another mentor of mine is a seminary professor named Randy Woodley. Randy is Cherokee.

He is a husband and a father, he cares for a whole community of indigenous and white co-journeyers on his farm outside of a small Oregon town, and he is my friend.

When I told Randy about this book, his response was quick and sober: "God cannot be hidden. Jesus cannot be hidden, only misunderstood."

When Randy says stuff like this, with his long grey ponytail and pendant of conk shell, it is hard for me not to lean in, hoping to hear more. He chooses each word with care. His hands rise and fall in front of him, beating with the rhythm of his words.

Not long ago, we spent an afternoon together in his home, sitting in front of his potbellied stove. It seemed appropriate to sit together in casual and careful conversation around a fire. Through the afternoon, I rarely spoke. I didn't want to. Randy gave, and he gave his thoughts on God. I will try to recount here some of what he said. I pray I do justice to his words.

Randy began like this, "In the New Testament, Jesus is called 'Creator' five times. Each of those times it is in the context of a hymn or a poem. When they are spoken, it is like they are memorized, the oral telling of the most essential beliefs in our Jesus-faith."

> In the beginning was the Word,
> And the Word was with God,
> And the Word was God . . .
> All things came into being through Him,
> And apart from Him nothing came into being
> That has come into being.
> In Him was life,
> And the life was the Light of men.
> The Light shines in the darkness,
> And the darkness did not comprehend it. (John 1:1–5 NASB)

> He is the image of the invisible God,
> The firstborn of all creation.
> For by Him all thing were created,
> Both in the heavens and on earth,
> Visible and invisible,
> Whether thrones or dominions
> Or rulers or authorities—
> All things have been created through Him
> And for Him.
> He is before all things,
> And in Him all things hold together. (Col. 1:15–17 NASB)

Randy continued, "Jesus is more than just Creator, creating from a distance. The language of our faith is clear. The Spirit of the Creator is in all things, in the DNA of all. Christ the Word is holding all things together. You can go as far as you can imagine out into the multiverse (beyond the universe), and Jesus is. You can go as far as you can imagine down into the subatomic, and Jesus is.

"The Creator, who is Trinity, is present in all, as we are taught in Romans 1. When the sun is on my face, there is the Creator. It is the 'unity in diversity' of the Trinity that makes the unity in diversity of all things possible. And that is Shalom, the peace of God.

"Christ calls us to his Shalom-kingdom, and not as an abstraction. He invites us to live it out. He says to us, 'Taste and see.'"

Randy didn't stop there. He spoke about tragedy and pain, not to explain them away but to explore the intended unity of all things. He spoke about humanity's foolishness and loss of harmony with creation and how those realities undermine our experience of Shalom.

I felt like I was only grasping the misty edges of what Randy was sharing. While he was speaking, and more so on my long drive back home, I was reflecting on the numerous obstacles that separate me from an integrated Creator-life (connecting to the Creator who is in all things, as it says, "In Him all things are held together").

It seems that my life has conspired to keep me from creation integration.

I have never known what it is to have a necessary and expectant relationship with the animals that I eat; I only know them wrapped in cellophane. I have never run after or alongside my food or seen them as coparticipants in the divine story.

I have never experienced the seasons (spring, summer, autumn, winter) as my rich friends or fierce foes. For me a harsh winter is only an inconvenience, not a potential death sentence. A drought means my vegetables might cost me a few cents more at the supermarket. I have no concept of shared groaning with my nonhuman neighbors (or human for that matter). I also have no concept of the celebration that comes from an unexpectedly abundant harvest.

I have no real relationship with the weather. For instance, most of the houses I have lived in were built on ancient floodplains, like the fool who Jesus said did not build his house up on the rock. If I were honest, I have more of a relationship with the Corps of Engineers than I do with ever-possible floodwaters.

These examples and a thousand other mental and lifestyle obstacles have isolated me from creation integration. I have been told all my life that I can go for a hike, enjoy a fishing weekend, or visit the ocean in order to engage God through creation, but isn't that really just creation-tourism (and Creator-tourism)?

If I have "misunderstood" God, as Randy warned, maybe part of my problem is that my life of comfort, my overintegration with the mostly human-built world, and my addiction to the immediate, the entertaining, and the convenient have blocked my view of the Creator who is in all things.

In our times together, Randy and I have gone round and round about innumerable topics, conversations I wish I could replay for you now. I do want to share one more idea with you from our time together that day, sitting around his potbellied stove.

Randy said to me, "We need to reconsider our entire image of

God. God is love, and love is vulnerable. God may be the most vulnerable being in the universe. God is as vulnerable as . . . as . . . as the eye of a snail." As he said it, he held up one hand flat as if a snail were perched upon it, and with the index finger of his other hand, he pantomimed pocking the snail's eye. His finger would then recoil when the imaginary eye retracted from his touch.

"God is more gentle than a nursing mother. Or think about this, what could be more vulnerable than the father in the story of the prodigal son? He allowed his son to hurt him and take from him. With his strength, the father should have disowned him. But instead, he watched the horizon. The language suggests that every day he was watching, because when the son was still a 'long way off, [he] saw him . . . and embraced him and kissed him.'[1]

"God cannot be hidden. Jesus cannot be hidden, only misunderstood.

"And here is the amazing thing. If we can truly come to believe that Jesus, the Creator, is in all things, then he can also hide in all things. He can hide in the words of a Muslim, a Buddhist . . . in street folk, in protestors . . . and even in Communist scholars. Jesus is the Truth; all streams of truth flow out of and into him."

Each morning, when Randy wakes, he goes to find some water. In the tradition of the Cherokee people, he splashes water on his face four times and prays, "God help me this day. Help me to walk in a good way."

Then he goes outside and holds his hands up to the sun and prays to the Triune Creator. He refers to God with a word from his people's language. That word is *Oo-nay-tla-nah-hee*. Translated into English, it means, "The One Behind Everything."

Beginnings and Endings by Jonathan Case

CONCLUSION
BEGINNINGS AND ENDINGS

"If I find in myself a desire which no experience in this world can satisfy, the most probable explanation is that I was made for another world."
—C. S. LEWIS, *MERE CHRISTIANITY*

WHAT AM I TO do with a God who hides? I have a hunger for God that I cannot shake. Try as I might to run away, I cannot.

I have a thirst for drink and have been given a world full of water.

I have a hunger for food and the varieties of sustenance are never-ending.

I have a need for air and all I must do is expand my lungs.

I have a longing for rest and only need close my eyes.

I have an aching for love and I simply must find my way home.

I have an essential yearning for God and yet where . . . how?

Maybe Lewis was right. Maybe I was simply made for "another world."

———

This book began with the story of my nephew Ransom, who was diagnosed with a most insidious and debilitating sort of cancer. It was his unimaginable and inexplicable sickness and my desire for God to be with him in his pain and chaos that sent me on this journey of God-exploration. In a very real way, a four-year-old commissioned me to write, and here I sit, at book's end.

Ransom, I have questioned my story as deeply as I know how, and yet I have not found any assurances or formulas, but here is some of what I believe God is inviting me to believe.

God hides. It is just a reality.

Sure, there are the unexpected moments of divine tangibility. There was the voice from heaven that told Abraham to stay his hand and not kill Isaac. There was the still small voice to Elijah in the cave of Mount Horeb, and there was Saul's Damascus road. In my story there have been a few moments, just moments, over my forty-plus years, when God's presence was more than just suspicious, more than just longing or coincidence. There was my Grandma's family room, and there was a lost day in my Macedonian bedroom. The rest is soaked in inference and hope.

That may simply be God's way. God has created a system of mostly silence. The gaps are so wide that we cannot help but be shocked by the moments when God does surprise. My Bible even describes seasons wherein generations upon generations experience heavenly silence. Can I accept my place in this harmonious story of faith?

Ironically, there is possibly no greater evidence of God's hiddenness than the incarnation of Jesus. Yes, we believe that Jesus is God's great revealing: divine character manifested in flesh and blood. However, it was also the most elaborate form of hiding in all of human history. God, the Eternal One, the Creator of heaven and earth, the one who "holds all things together," was conflated into a walking-talking pile of meat. It is like trying to get a down sleeping bag into a stuff-bag; the only difference is that this sleeping bag is larger than the universe. If that is not the greatest game of hide-and-seek, I don't know what is. God literally walked down the streets of Palestine, and people simply didn't notice. The Divine shopped for bread and was flippantly told to wait his turn. The Provider had to ask a kid to give up his lunch. The Creator of volcanoes and supernovas took on betrayal and denial from his best friends. The Eternal King was spat upon. The Vengeful was punched and punched, and whipped and tortured, and pierced and hung and stabbed and in the end only offered, "Forgive them, they know not what they do."

That is what I mean by hidden! God hides—scandalous, scandalous hiding. And what do I do? I petulantly complain. But that is me . . . I am weak. It doesn't surprise God. God knows me. He loves me. He loves me enough to receive my petulance, hold my doubt, and accept my weakness, so much so that God even leaves me breadcrumbs along the way. It seems that God, for some eternal reason, does not want my faith to be easy, but God is also committed to helping me not wander too far from the Way. For that I am thankful.

Sometimes I think that half the solution is just having the freedom to say what I feel, to articulate what I experience (or what I don't experience), and to do so within a community of faith that, coincidentally, believes we are all weak, broken, and needy. Isn't that the "gospel" after all?

What if we actually radically practiced the gospel? What if we started to admit that we are needy? What if we started to actually believe that our hope is not in our "experience" or in the fact that we have "figured it out," nor is it found in our triumphalistic language? Ultimately, our hope is found in God. It is God's work in us and in the world, whether I am aware of it or not.

Now, this journey has taught me something else about God. It is true that God hides. God hid in the incarnation. God hides in the silent Spirit. The Scriptures even say, "We look not to what is seen, but to what is unseen, for what is seen is temporal, but what is unseen is eternal."[1]

But it is more than that . . .

God also hid from me inside my Grandma and her canon of stories.

God hid from me inside and through my childhood imaginations.

God hid from me inside a wolverine, a mime, and dozens of strangers on my Smallville college campus.

God hid from me inside Kevin, Patrick, Erin, and Andy.

God hid from me inside my adventures and in my fears.

God hid from me inside the tragic death of a twenty-one-year-old named Layne, in a campus prayer vigil, and in a fraternity full of friends waiting to be discovered.

God hid from me inside my pioneer-dad, my Albania mission, and yes, even my fatal flaws.

God hid from me inside a Greek ambassador and a Cold War telephone.

God hid from me inside people smuggling and a Parisian angel.

God hid from me inside my self-destruction and my tragic failures.

God hid inside a seminary classroom and inside a beer hall.

And ironically, God hides from me equally inside my times of "faith" and my times of selfishness and doubt.

And today . . .

God hides from me inside my sister's sorrow.

God hides from me inside my Uncle Larry and my Uncle Richard.

God hides from me inside the mundane and the exceptional.

God hides from me inside my family and all around my neighborhood.

God hides from me inside a Cascade forest and a Cherokee's words.

God hides from me in the stories of a Divine King who touched lepers,
    loved the poor,
    befriended sinners,
    told stories,

instructed to love,

honored strangers,

embraced the marginalized,

pitched tables,

kneeled with basin and towel,

served bread and wine,

received spittle and spear,

said, "Lord forgive them . . ."

gave up breath,

loves on,

and who hid inside my Grandma and her canon of stories.

It was Ransom who unknowingly commissioned the writing of this book. I wanted God to be with him. I wanted God to be tangibly present. I wanted God to hold his hand.

As his loving uncle, I also wanted to be his teacher. I wanted to be able to reassure him about the things of God. I wanted to be able to tell him that I was confident that God would comfort him and, Lord forbid, walk with him through death.

In the end, I never got a chance.

On March 25, 2013, after four years and 311 days under the sun, Ransom died. He passed during the writing of this book.

I wanted these musings to be a gift to him, but instead he has given the gift to me. He has allowed me to journey back through the story of my life and catalog the tales of my suspicious encounters with God and the seasons of aching silence. Like happens so often in the kingdom of God, the tables have turned. I wanted to be the giver but became the receiver. I wanted to be the strong one yet I was replaced by the weak. I wanted to be the teacher yet became the student.

It has been a gift.

I pray that you, too, have found yourself curating anew your own museum of memories.

I wanted to be Ransom's teacher, but instead he has become mine. For now, I am still left with my questions, doubts, and confusions.

Today, Ransom is on a different path, far different from mine. For him, faith has become sight. I wish he could come to the table and share with us now. He would have much to show us.

The question of God's tangible presence is no longer a mystery to Ransom.

He has passed from death unto life. And I believe that God is holding his hand.

SCRIPTURE REFERENCES

INTRODUCTION
1. Luke 3:22, paraphrase

CHAPTER 2
1. Matthew 18:3, paraphrase
2. John 5:19 NIV

CHAPTER 4
1. Acts 8:18–20 NASB
2. Matthew 19:16 NASB
3. Matthew 7:21–23 NASB

CHAPTER 5
1. Luke 10:27, paraphrase
2. Matthew 13:34–35 MSG
3. Luke 17:2 NIV

CHAPTER 7
1. NASB

CHAPTER 8
1. Hebrews 4:12 NKJV

CHAPTER 9
1. NIV

CHAPTER 13
1. John 10:9 NASB

CHAPTER 14
1. Romans 15:19 NIV

CHAPTER 16
1. Acts 16:6–10 NASB, emphasis mine

CHAPTER 18
1. NASB
2. Psalm 23:1–5 NASB
3. Matthew 6:9–13 NASB

CHAPTER 19
1. NIV
2. See Ruth 4:13–15

3. See John 2:1–11
4. See Matthew 25:1–13
5. See Luke 14:7–11, Matthew 22:1–14

CHAPTER 20
1. John 16:7, 13 NASB

CHAPTER 22
1. Paraphrase

CHAPTER 23
1. NIV

CHAPTER 24
1. NIV
2. 2 Corinthians 5:2, paraphrase

CHAPTER 25
1. Luke 15:20 NASB

CONCLUSION
1. 2 Corinthians 4:18, paraphrase

KICKSTARTER CONTRIBUTORS

Deb Stuart
Austin Davidsen
Maria Rippo
Scott Blair
Susan Grow-Brecko
Rev. James A. Goins
W. Elizabeth Chapin
Lori Taylor
Shaun Sheahan
Brian Morrissette
Kari Gale
David and Laurie
    Quigley
Some Guy Who Likes
    Tony
The Austins
Cary Umhau
Don and Kathryn
    Mansfield
Bryan Johnson
    Family
Nicholas Edwards
    Park
Jay Beaman
David LaMotte
Team Treadway
Daniel Wendler
Jeremy Robinson
Jason Terwee
Susan Schaefer
K. Twiss

Dave and Karen
    Knudtson
Amberfry
Dr. Matt and Farron
Friday Morning
    Group
Mrs. Jones :)
Emily Crawford
Kyle and Brooke
    Fenton
Harriet Reed
    Congdon
Denise West
Sister Elle
Athanasius and
    Ambrose Hardesty
Sean Power
Tim Soerens
David Wise
Phil Long
Nils Ringo
Scott and Jojo
Brigid Brink
Beth Anderson
Frances McGaugh
Jeremy M Fortner
Mark and Maggie
    Dahl
Noel and Karyn
    Thurston
Kriz Family

John and Kate
    Pattison
The Harris Family
David and Lorie Beall
Stacy Gorton
Jeremiah and Hannah
    Meeks
Dawn Stenberg
Mark Portrait
Summer Miller
Todd and Sara Price
Greg Englund
Christian Piatt
Sean Hall
Nathan and Brooke
    Bubna
Gary and Mary
    Schulstad
Denys Hartsfield
Clark Blakeman
KC and Micky Jones
Brad Buchholz
Kristine Sommer
Jonathan Ortiz Myers
Nicole Shaffer
Evan Swanson
Bradley Swope
Patti Bauman
    Widener
Treama Simmons
    Marvel

ACKNOWLEDGMENTS

WHERE ELSE IS THERE to begin than to thank my phenomenal wife, our boys, our communal household, our community, and our neighbors. Thank you, all.

I am also grateful for my sister, her husband, Clint, their boys, and the role they have played in the writing of this book.

Ransom, we thank you for your life.

Sometimes writing a book is as much about the places where you write as it is about the places you write about. My glorious home of Portland, Oregon, is full of such places. I am thankful for the Grotto prayer chapel and the Tower of Cosmic Reflections at the Lan Su Chinese Gardens. I am thankful for Alex at the Detention Bar and for Cait and the crew that runs the basement space at Kell's Irish Pub. These places and many more provided the stage for this work of storytelling.

This book is quite full of the people who have been with me through my chapters of chaos and clarity. There are so very many . . . here are a few: Grandma, my Ecuador leaders, my pastors, Vavs, Caroline, Patrick, Kevin, Ms. Ward, Marty, Michelle, Layne, Wilson,

Sigma Pi fraternity, Geni, Todd, Philippe, Don, "Ministry Leader", Josh, Bryan, and Randy.

Special thanks to Jonathan Case for partnering with us on this project. Your artwork has set this book apart.

I leaned on a whole group of talented and opinionated folks in the creation of this manuscript. Much love and appreciation to Sean, Elizabeth, Micky, Philip, Karyn, James, Jeremiah, Jefferson, Nils, Patrick, Ovi, Faithna, Brandon, and many others. Special thanks to Jeff Martin, who is not only one of my closest friends but a seemingly unending source of encouragement and support.

Amy Gorenca and Philip Cox contributed dozens and dozens of hours to lovingly support and promote this project.

Emotionally and spiritually, I am thankful to three groups in particular during the season of writing this book. The first is my Friday circle: a diverse group of friends who lovingly (and often caustically) look out for me. My fellow instructors and colleagues at Warner Pacific College (*www.warnerpacific.edu*)—particularly our President, Andrea Cook. Finally, The Parish Collective (*www.parishcollective. org*), the most inspiring collection of faith practitioners and friends: "Rooted and Linked."

I would like to end this short expression of gratitude by saying thank you and "see you later" to my dear friend and mentor, Richard Twiss. Uncle Richard died during the writing of this book. Hardly a day goes by where his name is not mentioned amongst my family or community. His unique and unwavering belief in me as a human, a scholar, and a voice for the Jesus-Way was one of the great gifts of my life. Uncle Richard, I am, in many ways, lost without you. I will always miss you.

Blessings, dear friends . . . and grow where you are planted.

ABOUT THE AUTHOR

TONY IS HUSBAND TO Aimee, father to three courageous and creative boys, unofficial ambassador of his beloved Portland, devoted to his neighborhood, honored by his communal household, and a friend to the religious and irreligious alike.

He is the Author in Residence at Warner Pacific College. He teaches there and beyond on topics of authentic faith, spiritual formation, cultural integration, cross-spiritual communication, and sacred friendship.

His writing life involves books (including *Neighbors and Wise Men*), articles (including *Leadership Journal*), and playful profundity through his blog (www.tonykriz.com).

How did he get here? He was raised by Skip and Susie in the theatrical town of Eugene, Oregon. He spent his young adulthood in the developing world, including two years living with and being loved by a Muslim family in Albania. He has learned the gospel alongside nonreligious barflies and undergrad geniuses at places like Reed College. He has stumblingly submitted himself to his diverse household, to multicultural communities, and to those passionate about a rebirth of parish passion (www.parishcollective.org).

Through words, both written and spoken, Tony hopes to give people permission to authentically feel/speak/struggle and to honestly express their faith-filled affections.

Let the epiphanies come.

ABOUT THE ILLUSTRATOR

JONATHAN CASE IS AN artist and writer based in Portland, Oregon. His work includes the graphic novel, *Dear Creature*, art for DC's *Batman '66*, and multiple Dark Horse Comics titles including the Eisner Award-winning *Green River Killer* (with Jeff Jensen), *The Creep* (with John Arcudi), and others.

http://jonathancase.net